# PROGRESS IN 1896.

THE advance toward the full solution of the problem of manflight which was made in the year 1896 was greater than that of any previous year. Saving the sad death of Lilienthal, the chronicler's pen has only good news to tell.

In times past the extreme difficulty of determining what were the best methods of work was the deterrent which kept investigators from entering the field of aeronautics, and consequently the world's workers were comparatively small in number.

Now, this condition of affairs no longer obtains, for the demonstrations of 1896 were such that the best lines for investigators to follow are very clearly marked out. These lines, three in number, distinct, yet convergent, are as follows:

1. The development of the self-propelled aerodrome.
2. The development of the motorless air-sailer.
3. The development of the motor.

In each of these departments of work there is now a well-defined point of vantage which is accessible to every intelligent experimenter who is inclined to carefully study the ground already traversed, and so to fully understand the results already reached.

Whichever branch of work is seriously undertaken by an individual, he may be sure that, while working upon his own specialty, he is helping those engaged in others toward their common goal.

As stated in the first number of THE ANNUAL, if this compilation should happily bring any new workers into the field of aeronautical experiment, the hopes of the editor will be amply fulfilled.

*Plate I.*

SAMUEL PIERPONT LANGLEY, Ph.D., LL.D., D.C.L.,

Secretary of the Smithsonian Institution.

From a photograph taken at Oxford in 1891.

# The

# Aeronautical Annual.

## 1897.

DEVOTED TO THE ENCOURAGEMENT OF EXPERIMENT WITH AERIAL
MACHINES, AND TO THE ADVANCEMENT OF THE
SCIENCE OF AERODYNAMICS.

EDITED BY

# JAMES MEANS.

The American publishers will send this number, postpaid, to any
address on receipt of one dollar.

BOSTON, MASS.:

## W. B. CLARKE & CO.,

PARK ST., COR. TREMONT ST.

LONDON:

## WILLIAM WESLEY & SON,

28 ESSEX ST., STRAND.

## American Aeronautical Archives

Published by Markowski International Publishers
One Oakglade Circle, Hummelstown, PA 17036
American Aeronautical Archives is an imprint of
Markowski International Publishers
www.AeronauticalPublishers.com

This Markowski edition is an unabridged facsimile of the original work, compiled and edited by James Means, and first published in 1897 then in 2003 in Celebration of the Centennial of Flight. It includes all the original aeronautical photographs and illustrations. The Foreword to the Markowski Edition was specially prepared for this edition.

Publisher's Cataloguing-in-Publication

Means, James, Editor, 1853-1920
  The Aeronautical Annual 1897: Foreword by Michael A. Markowski, p.cm.
  Originally published in Boston, Massachusetts by W.B. Clarke & Co., 1897
  ISBN: 978-0-938716-97-6

  1.  Flying Machine—History.  2. Aeronautics—History
  I.  Title

# To the Memory

OF THOSE WHO,

INTELLIGENTLY BELIEVING IN THE POSSIBILITY

OF

## MECHANICAL FLIGHT,

HAVE

LIVED DERIDED,

AND

DIED IN SORROW AND OBSCURITY

# FOREWORD

*The Aeronautical Annuals* of 1895-96-97 are among the most important pre-Wright era aviation books ever published. Prized by collectors, original editions are extremely rare; a pristine original set could be worth $3,000. In tribute to the brave early aviation pioneers, I am delighted to re-publish these treasures and make them available to everyone.

In a letter to James Means's son, Philip, dated November 12, 1921, Orville Wright wrote: "*The Aeronautical Annuals* of 1895-96-97 contained the best collection of reprints from the work of the earlier experimenters in aviation…, and I do not know of a better collection today. Your father showed rare good judgment in his selections, separating most of the good work from the mass of worthless matter which had been published.

"Your father's work was of great benefit to us, and I think of my personal acquaintance with him with affection."

After stumbling upon an original set of these amazing books in 1972 in an old, out-of-the-way bookstore in Boston, with Tom Peghiny, my first student and great friend ever since, I committed to advancing ultralight aviation. Tom went on to become a world champion hangglider pilot, maker of ultralight aircraft, and founder of light sport aircraft leader Flight Design USA. These three books, along with Otto Lilienthal's landmark *Birdflight as the Basis of Aviation,* inspired me to leave my job as an aerospace engineer to design and manufacture hanggliders. I then wrote *The Hang Glider's Bible*, and started publishing books.

In 1899 the Smithsonian recommended the *Annuals* to Wilbur Wright when he wrote asking for information on human flight. These three volumes are books of vision, featuring the plans, dreams, and schemes of some of aviation's visionaries—Da Vinci, Cayley, Henson, Langley, Maxim, Herring, Chanute, Lilienthal, and others.

The *Annuals* provided the Wrights with a wealth of knowledge about the thinking and experiments which had been done up until that time, giving them a foundation on which to formulate their own ideas. Each volume is packed with incredible information, drawings, and photographs of the pre-Wright era, making them must-reads for all aviation enthusiasts.

Blue skies and tailwinds,
— *Mike Markowski*

# CONTENTS.

|  |  | Page |
|---|---|---|
| I. | SAMUEL PIERPONT LANGLEY | 5 |
| II. | STORY OF EXPERIMENTS IN MECHANICAL FLIGHT<br>By S. P. Langley. | 11 |
| III. | THE AERODROMES IN FLIGHT | 26 |
| IV. | AERODROME NO. 5, '96 | 29 |
| V. | RECENT EXPERIMENTS IN GLIDING FLIGHT<br>By Octave Chanute. | 30 |
| VI. | RECENT ADVANCES TOWARD A SOLUTION OF THE PROBLEM OF THE CENTURY<br>By A. M. Herring. | 54 |
| VII. | OTTO LILIENTHAL. A Memorial Address<br>By Karl Müllenhoff. | 75 |
| VIII. | OUR TEACHERS IN SAILING FLIGHT<br>By Otto Lilienthal. | 84 |
| IX. | AT RHINOW<br>By Otto Lilienthal. | 92 |
| X. | THE BEST SHAPES FOR WINGS<br>By Otto Lilienthal. | 95 |
| XI. | SAILING FLIGHT. (Conclusion.) Begun in No. 2<br>By Octave Chanute. | 98 |
| XII. | THE WAY OF AN EAGLE IN THE AIR<br>By E. C. Huffaker. | 128 |
| XIII. | SCREW-PROPELLERS WORKING IN AIR<br>By Hiram S. Maxim. | 142 |
| XIV. | GLIDING EXPERIMENTS<br>By Percy S. Pilcher. | 144 |
| XV. | MISCELLANY<br>Carbonic Acid or Air. — Professor Zahm's Experiments. — Blue Hill Aerial Explorations. — A Keel Kite. — A Rubber-propelled Model. — Methods of launching Aerial Machines. — The Albatross. — Plates XVII. and XVIII. — The Secret. — Blue Hill Measurements of the Velocity of Flying Ducks, etc., etc. | 147 |
| XVI. | EDITORIAL<br>The Scientific Value of Flying Models. — Motive Power for Flying Models. — An Important Work. — Koch's Apparatus, etc., etc. | 161 |

# LIST OF PLATES.

Plate

I. PORTRAIT OF SAMUEL PIERPONT LANGLEY . *Frontispiece*

II. SCALE DRAWINGS OF LANGLEY'S AERODROME
NO. 5 . *To face page* 26

III. LANGLEY'S AERODROME IN FLIGHT 28

IV. GLIDING MACHINES . 34

V. CHANUTE'S GLIDING MACHINE IN FLIGHT 36

VI. GLIDING MACHINES . 38

VII. WORKING DRAWING OF CHANUTE'S GLIDING MACHINE . 40

VIII. GLIDING MACHINES . 42

IX. LAUNCHING WAYS, ETC. 48

X. CAMP CHANUTE AND BLUE HILL OBSERVATORY 50

XI. HERRING'S APPARATUS 64

XII. EQUILIBRIUM PARADOX, ETC. 66

XIII. GLIDING MACHINE AND MOTOR 68

XIV. WORKING DRAWING OF GLIDING MACHINE 72

XV. GLIDING MACHINE IN FLIGHT 74

XVI. PORTRAIT OF OTTO LILIENTHAL . 76

XVII. MISCELLANY. WING MECHANISM 156

XVIII. MISCELLANY. WING CONTOURS AND MUSCLES 156

# SAMUEL PIERPONT LANGLEY.

SAMUEL PIERPONT LANGLEY [1] was born in Roxbury, Mass., on Aug. 22, 1834. At the age of eleven he entered the Boston Latin School, and afterward the English High School, graduating from that excellent institution in 1851, after completing the usual three years' course. As his inclinations tended strongly to mathematical and mechanical pursuits he was not sent to college, and at that time none of the opportunities of higher scientific education now existing at the Massachusetts-Institute of Technology and other similar institutions of learning were available for the young student. From his early youth he had been deeply interested in everything pertaining to astronomy, and with the aid of his brother had constructed several small telescopes for the study of the heavens. After leaving the English High School he entered the office of an architect in Boston, and in 1857 commenced the practice of his profession at the West, in Chicago and St. Louis.

The financial and political troubles of the period just before the civil war interfered so seriously with success that he returned to Boston in 1864, occupying the next year with a journey to Europe with his brother. On his return, congenial occupation offered itself in the shape of an appointment as assistant to Prof. Joseph Winlock, then director of the Harvard Observatory.

This opportunity of doing real astronomical work was eagerly seized, and led the next year (1866) to his appointment as assistant professor of mathematics at the U.S. Naval Academy, where in the intervals of arduous work he put in order the small observatory established by Prof. William Chauvenet.

The next year he accepted the appointment of director of

---

1 Abridged by Commander Francis M. Green, U.S.N., from the advanced sheets of a memoir of the three secretaries of the Smithsonian Institution.

the observatory and professor of astronomy and physics at the Western University of Pennsylvania, and in connection with this appointment was director of the Alleghany Observatory, then an observatory only in name, consisting of a building in which was a thirteen-inch equatorial without either a clock, transit, or chronograph, and entirely devoid of either a library or endowment.

To raise money for the equipment of the observatory and to enable him to prosecute original research, an admirable scheme was devised by Mr. Langley by which exact time was transmitted by telegraph twice a day to all the principal stations of the Pennsylvania Railway from the observatory. This was the introduction on a large scale of the system of time distribution from observatories which has since become universal. By this means about eight thousand miles of railway were eventually run by these time-signals, affording altogether during the administration of Mr. Langley more than sixty thousand dollars devoted entirely to the uses of the observatory.

The time-service and the resulting income becoming regularly established, the work of research upon the solar atmosphere was commenced and carried on energetically in spite of great difficulties.

The seventeen years from 1870 to 1887 were productive of most excellent and striking work in the study of solar physics. The limits of this sketch only permit this work to be briefly referred to, but astronomers of all nations have united in eulogizing the skill, devotion, and tireless perseverance which have given to the world the intensely interesting and valuable information regarding the heat, light, and chemical action due to the solar radiation.

In his study of the sun's heat he found that the thermopile effectively used for nearly fifty years was not sufficiently sensitive and trustworthy, and this difficulty led Mr. Langley to the invention of the bolometer. By this instrument very small amounts of radiant heat may be measured, changes of temperature of less than $\frac{1}{100000}$ of a degree F. being accurately indicated. Its action is based on the variations of electrical resistance produced by changes of temperature in a metallic conductor, like a minute strip of platinum. This strip forms one arm of an electric balance, the change in the strength of the current flowing through it being measured by a delicate galvanometer.[1] This beautiful instrument has recently been made more effective by the invention of the bolograph, which photographically records the fluctuations of the galvanometer needle. With these instruments Mr. Langley may·be said to have opened up a new department of physics.

Mr. Langley's contributions to science have been numerous, and are to be found in the scientific journals of this country and of Europe. Besides these, the "Century Magazine" in 1884 and 1886 contained a series of popular articles on astrophysical research based on lectures delivered by him at the Lowell Institute in 1883. These articles have been since republished in book form under the title of "The New Astronomy," a most fascinating and successful work.

In 1887 he was chosen by the lamented Spencer F. Baird, already in failing health, as his assistant in the secretaryship of the Smithsonian Institution, and in the same year after the death of Professor Baird he was elected secretary of the Smithsonian Institution.

Interested from boyhood in the problems of aerial flight as illustrated by soaring birds, it was not till 1889 that he found opportunity for serious work in this direction. In 1891 he published his now famous memoir entitled "Experiments in Aerodynamics," and in 1893 the equally celebrated one on "The Internal Work of the Wind." The importance of the views thus advanced was universally admitted as shown by able articles by various experts, notably Mr. O. Chanute, of Chicago, Dr. von Salverda, of Holland, and Lt.-Col. Elsdale, of the Royal Engineers. Satisfied that important results would be derived from continued experimental work, Mr. Langley diligently prosecuted his investigations, and in May, 1896, he had the intense satisfaction of seeing an aerodrome constructed by him-

---

[1] "The Bolometer and Radiant Energy." Proceedings of the American Academy of Arts and Sciences, 1880–1881.

self make two successful flights, each to a distance of more than half a mile. A third and still longer flight was made on November 28 with another machine built of steel like the first, and like that driven by propellers actuated by a steam-engine.

Mr. Octave Chanute, of Chicago, on the 10th of April, 1896, wrote as follows:

In my judgment the principal contributions thus far made by Doctor Langley to the science of aerodynamics consist in his having given to physicists and searchers firm ground to stand upon concerning the fundamental and much-disputed question of air resistances and reaction.

When I was in Europe, in 1889, I inquired into the state of knowledge on this important question, and found utter disagreement and confusion. There were numerous formulæ, promoted by various physicists, but these gave such discordant results that arrangements were being proposed in France to try an entire set of new experiments, with air currents to be procured by an enormous fan-blower. A fair idea of the state of knowledge can be had from Professor Marey's careful work on "Le vol des oiseaux," published in 1890. Oblique pressures were then still generally held to vary according to the Newtonian law, or as the square of the sine of incidence, although this gives but five to ten per cent. of the true reactions at acute angles of incidence.

Doctor Langley has shown us, by experiment, the general accuracy of which cannot be questioned, that the empirical (based on experiments) formula of Duchemin is sufficiently correct to calculate the radiations upon planes; so that the French, who had ignored this formula since 1836, now claim its inception and accept it (as they do some wines) *retour d'Amérique*. Doctor Langley has also shown us that the variation of the centre of pressure on an inclined plane, observed by Sir George Cayley and by Avanzani as well as by Kummer, follows approximately the law formulated by Jossel, so that now, for the first time, searchers are enabled to calculate the sustaining power, the resistance, and the centre of pressure of a plane, with confidence that they are not far wrong; and this, together with the further law, formulated first by Doctor Langley, that within certain limits "the higher speeds are more economical of power than the lower ones," has made it possible to assert that the problem of artificial flight is not insoluble as theretofore affirmed by many of the most eminent scientific men.

Whether Doctor Langley's scientific labors in this department of physics will soon result, like those of the preceding secretaries, in the practical application of his discoveries to the use of mankind, it is perhaps too early to assert positively. I think, myself, that they will so result before many years, but there are so many intricate questions to be solved before commercial success can be achieved that another generation may pass before the problem of flight is fully solved.

Moreover, Doctor Langley's labors and discoveries are by no means over. He has thus far published only the result of his investigations on planes, while saying in the penultimate paragraph of his summary that it is not asserted that planes are the best forms to use. Lilienthal and Phillips have since shown that concave-convex surfaces are more efficient forms, and it is very much to be desired that Doctor Langley shall next publish some data concerning such forms.

The practical development of a scientific truth is somewhat like the growth from a new seed. We recognize the existence of the plant, we ascertain some of its virtues, but we cannot tell its full uses, how soon it will mature, nor how large the tree will be.

It is significant, however, that, prior to the publication of Doctor Langley's work, it was the rare exception to find engineers and scientists of recognized ability who would fully admit *the possibility* of man being able to solve the twenty-century-old problem of aviation. Prof. Joseph Le Conte, in the "Popular Science Monthly," of November, 1888, has very recently taken the ground, flatly, "that a pure flying-machine is impossible." This was probably based on the fact that the then accepted formula of Newton, and the calculation of Napier and other scientists, if correct, rendered the solution practically impossible. Since the publication of "Experiments in Aerodynamics," however, it is the exception to find an intelligent engineer who disputes the *probability* of the eventual solution of the problem of man-flight. Such has been the change in five years. Incredulity has given way, interest has been aroused in the scientific question, a sound basis has been furnished for experiment, and practical results are being evolved by many workers. Much remains to be discovered concerning curved surfaces, with which alone practical flight is likely to be achieved, but when this is accomplished it is probable, in my judgment, that the beginning of the solution will be acknowledged to date back to the publication of Doctor Langley's book, and that he will be distinguished as Secretary Henry is now with regard to the development of electrical appliances.

The administration of the Smithsonian Institution under the direction of Mr. Langley has been most satisfactory. Among the notable features of it have been the establishment of the National Zoölogical Park and the Smithsonian Astrophysical Observatory. The latter is an eminently fit object for endowment by an institution established to encourage research in physical science, especially as at the U.S. Naval Observatory at Washington none of the appropriated funds for its support are permitted to be used for physical research.

Mr. Langley's contributions to science have been numerous and have been largely published in the "Comptes Rendus" of the French Academy and in the "American Journal of Science."

Mr. Langley is a member of the National Academy of Sciences, a fellow of the Royal Astronomical Society, of the Royal Society of London, is an official correspondent of the French Academy, and a member of numerous other American and foreign scientific societies. In 1886 he was elected president of the American Association for the Advancement of Science. He has received the following honorary degrees: LL.D. from University Wisconsin in 1882, University Michigan in 1883, Harvard University in 1886, and Princeton University, 1896; D.C.L. from the University of Oxford in 1894. He was the first to receive from the National Academy of Sciences the Henry Draper medal for work in astronomical physics, and in 1887 was awarded the Rumford medal by the Royal Society of London, the Rumford gold and silver medals by the American Academy of Arts and Sciences.

More than all these formal honors by far is the world-wide recognition of his achievements in the discovery of so much of the solar spectrum and in the formulation of the principles of aerodynamics.

# STORY OF EXPERIMENTS IN MECHANICAL FLIGHT.

By Samuel Pierpont Langley.

THE Editor of " The Annual " has asked me to give matter of a somewhat personal nature for a narrative account of my work in aerodromics.

The subject of flight interested me as long ago as I can remember anything, but it was a communication from Mr. Lancaster, read at the Buffalo meeting of the American Association for the Advancement of Science, in 1886, which aroused my then dormant attention to the subject. What he said contained some remarkable but apparently mainly veracious observations on the soaring bird, and some more or less paradoxical assertions, which caused his communication to be treated with less consideration than it might otherwise have deserved. Among these latter was a statement that a model, somewhat resembling a soaring bird, wholly inert, and without any internal power, could, nevertheless, under some circumstances advance against the wind without falling; which seemed to me then, as it did to members of the Association, an utter impossibility, but which I have since seen reason to believe is, within limited conditions, theoretically possible.

I was then engaged in the study of astro-physics at the Observatory in Allegheny, Pennsylvania. The subject of mechanical flight could not be said at that time to possess any literature, unless it were the publications of the French and English aeronautical societies, but in these, as in everything then accessible, fact had not yet always been discriminated from fancy. Outside of these, almost everything was even less trustworthy; but though after I had experimentally demonstrated certain facts, anticipations of them were found by others on historical research, and though we can now distinguish in retrospective examination what would have been useful to the investigator if he had known it to be true, there was no test of the kind to apply at the time. I went to work, then, to find out for myself, and in my own way, what amount of mechanical power was requisite to sustain a given weight in the air, and make it advance at a given speed, for this seemed to be an inquiry which must necessarily precede any attempt at mechanical flight, which was the very remote aim of my efforts.

The work was commenced in the beginning of 1887 by the construction, at Allegheny, of a turn-table of exceptional size, driven by a steam-engine, and this was used during three years in making the "Experiments in Aerodynamics," which were published by the Smithsonian Institution, under that title, in 1891. Nearly all the conclusions reached were the result of direct experiment in an investigation which aimed to take nothing on trust. Few of them were then familiar, though they have since become so, and in this respect knowledge has advanced so rapidly that statements which were treated as paradoxical on my first enunciation of them are now admitted truisms.

It has taken me, indeed, but a few years to pass through the period when the observer hears that his alleged observation was a mistake; the period when he is told that if it were true, it would be useless; and the period when he is told that it is undoubtedly true, but that it has always been known.

May I quote from the introduction to this book what was said in 1891?

" I have now been engaged since the beginning of the year 1887 in experiments on an extended scale for determining the possibilities of, and the conditions for, transporting in the air a body whose specific gravity is greater than that of the air, and I desire to repeat my conviction that the obstacles in its way are not such as have been thought; that they lie more in such apparently secondary difficulties as those of guiding the body so that it may move in the direction desired, and ascend or descend with safety, than in what may appear to be the primary difficulties due to the nature of the air itself," and, I added, that in this field of research I thought that we were, at that time (only six years since), " in a relatively less advanced condition than the study of steam was before the time of Newcomen." It was also stated that the most important inference from those experiments as a whole was that mechanical flight was possible with engines we could then build, as one-horse power rightly applied could sustain over 200 pounds in the air at a horizontal velocity of somewhat over 60 feet a second.

As this statement has been misconstrued, let me point out that it refers to surfaces, used without guys, or other adjuncts, which would create friction; that the horse-power in question is that actually expended in the thrust, and that it is predicated only on a rigorously horizontal flight. This implies a large deduction from the power in the actual machine, where the brake horse-power of the engine, after a requisite allowance for loss in transmission to the propellers, and for their slip on the air, will probably be reduced to from one-half to one-quarter of its nominal amount; where there is great friction from the enforced use of guys and other adjuncts; but above all where there is no way to insure absolutely horizonal flight in free air. All these things allowed for, however, since it seemed to me possible to provide an engine which should give a horse-power for something like 10 pounds of weight, there was still enough to justify the statement that we possessed in the steam-engine, as then constructed, or in other heat engines, more than the indispensable power, though it was added that this was not asserting that a system of supporting surfaces could be securely guided through the air or safely brought to the ground, and that these and like considerations were of quite another order, and belonged to some inchoate art which I might provisionally call *aerodromics*.

These important conclusions were reached before the actual publication of the volume, and a little later others on the nature of the movements of air, which were published under the title of " The Internal Work of the Wind " (Smithsonian Contributions to Knowledge, Volume XXVII., 1893, No. 884). The latter were founded on experiments independent of the former, and which led to certain theoretical conclusions unverified in practice. Among the most striking and perhaps paradoxical of these, was that a suitably disposed free body might under certain conditions be sustained in an ordinary wind, and even advance against it without the expenditure of any energy from within.

The first stage of the investigation was now over, so far as that I had satisfied myself that mechanical flight was possible with the power we could hope to command, if only the art of directing that power could be acquired.

The second stage (that of the acquisition of this art) I now decided to take up. It may not be out of place to recall that at this time, only six years ago, a great many scientific men treated the whole subject with entire indifference as unworthy of attention or as outside of legitimate research, the proper field for the charlatan, and one on which it was scarcely prudent for a man with a reputation to lose, to enter.

The record of my attempts to acquire the art of flight may commence with the year 1889, when I procured a stuffed frigate bird, a California condor, and an albatross, and attempted to move them upon the whirling table at Allegheny. The experiments were very imperfect and the records are unfortunately lost, but the important conclusion to which they led was that a stuffed bird could not be made to soar except at speeds which were unquestionably very much greater than what served to sustain the living one, and the earliest experiments and all subsequent ones with actually flying models have shown that thus far we cannot carry nearly the weights which Nature does to a given sustaining surface, without a power much greater than she employs. At the time these experiments were begun, Penaud's ingenious but toy-like model was the only thing which could sustain itself in the air for even a few seconds, and calculations founded upon its performance sustained the conclusion that the amount of power required in actual free flight was far greater than that demanded by the theoretical enunciation. In order to learn under what conditions the aerodrome should be balanced for horizontal flight, I constructed over 30 modifications of the rubber-driven model, and spent many months in endeavoring from these to ascertain the laws of "balancing"; that is, of stability leading to horizontal flight. Most of these models had two propellers, and it was extremely difficult to build them light and strong enough. Some of them had superposed wings; some of them curved and some plane wings; in some the propellers were side by side, in others one propeller was at the front and the other at the rear, and so every variety of treatment was employed, but all were at first too heavy, and only those flew successfully which had from 3 to 4 feet of sustaining surface to a pound of weight, a proportion which is far greater than Nature employs in the soaring bird, where in some cases less than half a foot of sustaining surface is used to a pound. It had been shown in the "Experiments in Aerodynamics" that the centre of pressure on an inclined plane advancing was not at the centre of figure, but much in front of it, and this knowledge was at first nearly all I possessed in balancing these early aerodromes. Even in the beginning, also, I met remarkable difficulty in throwing them into the air, and devised numerous forms of launching apparatus which were all failures, and it was necessary to keep the construction on so small a scale that they could be cast from the hand.

The earliest actual flights with these were extremely irregular and brief, lasting only from three to four seconds. They were made at Allegheny in March, 1891, but these and all subsequent ones were so erratic and so short that it was possible to learn very little from them. Penaud states that he once obtained a flight of 13 seconds. I never got as much as this, but ordinarily little more than half as much, and came to the conclusion that in order to learn the art of mechanical flight it was necessary to have a model which would keep in the air for at any rate a longer period than these, and move more steadily. Rubber twisted in the way that Penaud used it, will practically give about 300 foot-pounds to a pound of weight, and at least as much must be allowed for the weight of the frame on which the rubber is strained. Twenty pounds of rubber and frame, then, would give 3,000 foot-pounds, or one-horse power for less than six seconds. A steam-engine, having apparatus for condensing its steam, weighing in all 10 pounds and carrying 10 pounds of fuel, would possess in this fuel, supposing that but one-tenth of its theoretical capacity is utilized, many thousand times the power of an equal weight of rubber, or at least one-horse power for some hours. Provided the steam could be condensed and the water re-used, then, the advantage of the steam over the spring motor was enormous, even in a model constructed only for the purpose of study. But the construction of a steam-driven aerodrome was too formidable a task to be undertaken lightly, and I examined the capacities of condensed air, carbonic acid gas, of various applications of electricity, whether in the primary or storage battery, of hot-water engines, of inertia motors, of the gas engine, and of still other material. The gas engine promised best of all in theory, but it was not yet developed in a suitable form. The steam-engine, as being an apparently familiar construction, promised best in practice, but in taking it up, I, to my cost, learned that in the special application to be made of it, little was really familiar and everything had to be learned by experiment. I had myself no previous knowledge of steam engineering, nor any assistants other than the very capable workmen employed. I well remember my difficulties over the first aerodrome (No. 0), when everything, not only the engine, but the boilers which were to supply it, the furnaces which were to heat it, the propellers which were to advance it, the hull which was to hold all these, — were all things to be originated, in a construction which, as far as I knew, had never yet been undertaken by any one.

It was necessary to make a beginning, however, and a compound engine was planned which, when completed, weighed about 4 pounds, and which could develop rather over a horse-power with 60 pounds of steam, which it was expected could be furnished by a series of tubular boilers arranged in " bee-hive" form, and the whole was to be contained in a hull about 5 feet in length and 10 inches in diameter. This hull was, as in the construction of a ship, to carry all adjuncts. In front of it projected a steel rod, or bowsprit, about its own length, and one still longer behind. The engines rotated two propellers, each about 30 inches in diameter, which were on the end of long shafts disposed at an acute angle to each other and actuated by a single gear driven from the engine. A single pair of large wings contained about 50 square feet, and a smaller one in the rear about half as much, or in all some 75 feet, of sustaining surface, for a weight which it was expected would not exceed 25 pounds.

Although this aerodrome was in every way a disappointment, its failure taught a great many useful lessons. It had been built on the large scale described, with very little knowledge of how it was to be launched into the air, but the construction developed the fact that it was not likely to be launched at all, since there was a constant gain in weight over the estimate at each step, and when the boilers were completed, it was found that they gave less than one-half the necessary steam, owing chiefly to the inability to keep up a proper fire. The wings yielded so as to be entirely deformed under a slight pressure of the air, and it was impossible to make them stronger without making them heavier, where the weight was already prohibitory. The engines could not transmit even what feeble power they furnished, without dangerous tremor in the long shafts, and there were other difficulties. When the whole approached completion, it was found to weigh nearer 50 pounds than 25, to develop only about one-half the estimated horsepower at the brake, to be radically weak in construction, owing to the yielding of the hull, and to be, in short, clearly a hopeless case.

The first steam-driven aerodrome had, then, proved a failure, and I reverted during the remainder of the year to simpler plans, among them one of an elementary gasolene engine.

I may mention that I was favored with an invitation from Mr. Maxim to see his great flying-machine at Bexley, in Kent, where I was greatly impressed with the engineering skill shown in its construction, but I found the general design incompatible with the conclusions that I had reached by experiments with small models, particularly as to what seemed to me advisable in the carrying of the centre of gravity as high as was possible with safety.

In 1892 another aerodrome (No. 1), which was to be used with carbonic acid gas, or with compressed air, was commenced. The weight of this aerodrome was a little over 4½ pounds, and the area of the supporting surfaces 6½ square feet. The engines developed but a small fraction of a horse-power, and they were able to give a dead lift of only about one-tenth of the weight of the aerodrome, giving relatively less power to weight than that obtained in the large aerodrome already condemned.

Toward the close of this year was taken up the more careful study of the position of the centre of gravity with reference to the line of thrust from the propellers, and to the centre of pressure. The centre of gravity was carried as high as was consistent with safety, the propellers being placed so high, with reference to the supporting wings, that the intake of air was partly from above and partly from below these latter. The lifting power (*i.e.*, the dead-lift) of the aerodromes was determined in the shop by a very useful contrivance which I have called the " pendulum," which consists of a large pendulum which rests on knife edges, but is prolonged above the points of support, and counterbalanced so as to present a condition of indifferent equilibrium. Near the lower end of this pendulum the aerodrome is suspended, and when power is applied to it, the reaction of the propellers lifts the pendulum through a certain angle. If the line of thrust passes through the centre of gravity, it will be seen that the sine of this angle will be the fraction of the weight lifted, and thus the dead-lift power of the engines becomes known. Another aerodrome was built, but both, however constructed, were shown by this pendulum test to have insufficient power, and the year closed with disappointment.

Aerodrome No. 3 was of stronger and better construction, and the propellers, which before this had been mounted on shafts inclined to each other in a **V**-like form, were replaced by parallel ones.   Boilers of the Serpolet type (that is, composed of tubes of nearly capillary section) were experimented with at great cost of labor and no results; and they were replaced with coil boilers.   For these I introduced, in April, 1893, a modification of the ælopile blast, which enormously increased the heat-giving power of the fuel (which was then still alcohol), and with this blast for the first time the boilers began to give steam enough for the engines.   It had been very difficult to introduce force pumps which would work effectively on the small scale involved, and after many attempts to dispense with their use by other devices, the acquisition of a sufficiently strong pump was found to be necessary in spite of its weight, but was only secured after long experiment.   It may be added that all the aerodromes from the very nature of their construction were wasteful of heat, the industrial efficiency little exceeding half of one per cent., or from one-tenth to one-twentieth that of a stationary engine constructed under favorable conditions.   This last aerodrome lifted nearly 30 per cent. of its weight upon the pendulum, which implied that it could lift much more than its weight when running on a horizontal track, and its engines were capable of running its 50-centimetre propellers at something over 700 turns per minute.   There was, however, so much that was unsatisfactory about it, that it was deemed best to proceed to another construction before an actual trial was made in the field, and a new aerodrome, designated as No. 4, was begun.   This last was an attempt, guided by the weary experience of preceding failures, to construct one whose engines should run at a much higher pressure than heretofore, and be much more economical in weight.   The experiments with the Serpolet boilers having been discontinued, the boiler was made with a continuous helix of copper tubing, which as first employed was about three millimetres internal diameter; and it may be here observed that a great deal of time was subsequently lost in attempts to construct a more advantageous form of boiler for the actual purposes than this simple one, which with a larger coil tube eventually proved to be the best; so that later constructions have gone back to this earlier type.   A great deal of time was lost in these experiments from my own unfamiliarity with steam engineering, but it may also be said that there was little help either from books or from counsel, for everything was here *sui generis*, and had to be worked out from the beginning. In the construction which had been reached by the middle of the third year of experiment, and which has not been greatly differed from since, the boiler was composed of a coil of copper in the shape of a hollow helix, through the centre of which the blast from the ælopile was driven, the steam and water passing into a vessel I called the " separator," whence the steam was led into the engines at a pressure of from 70 to 100 pounds (a pressure which has since been considerably exceeded).

From the very commencement of this long investigation the great difficulty was in keeping down the weight, for any of the aerodromes could probably have flown had they been built light enough, and in every case before the construction was completed the weight had so increased beyond the estimate, that the aerodrome was too heavy to fly, and nothing but the most persistent resolution kept me in continuing attempts to reduce it after further reduction seemed impossible. Toward the close of the year (1893) I had, however, finally obtained an aerodrome with mechanical power, as it seemed to me, to fly, and I procured, after much thought as to where this flight should take place, a small house-boat, to be moored somewhere in the Potomac; but the vicinity of Washington was out of the question, and no desirable place was found nearer than thirty miles below the city. It was because it was known that the aerodrome might have to be set off in the face of a wind, which might blow in any direction, and because it evidently was at first desirable that it should light in the water rather than on the land, that the house-boat was selected as the place for the launch. The aerodrome (No. 4) weighed between 9 and 10 pounds, and lifted 40 per cent. of this on the pendulum with 60 pounds of steam pressure, a much more considerable amount than was theoretically necessary for horizontal flight. And now the construction of a launching apparatus, dismissed for some years, was resumed. Nearly every form seemed to have been experimented with unsuccessfully in the smaller aerodromes. Most of the difficulties were connected with the fact that it is necessary for an aerodrome, as it is for a soaring bird, to have a certain considerable initial velocity before it can advantageously use its own mechanism for flight, and the difficulties of imparting this initial velocity with safety are surprisingly great, and in the open air are beyond all anticipation.

Here, then, commences another long story of delay and disappointment in these efforts to obtain a successful launch. To convey to the reader an idea of its difficulties, a few extracts from the diary of the period are given. (It will be remembered that each attempt involved a journey of thirty miles each way.)

Nov. 18, 1893. Having gone down to the house-boat, preparatory to the first launch, in which the aerodrome was to be cast from a springing piece beneath, it was found impossible to hold it in place on this before launching, without its being prematurely torn from its support, although there was no wind except a moderate breeze; and the party returned after a day's fruitless effort.

Two days later a relative calm occurred in the afternoon of a second visit, when the aerodrome was mounted again, but, though the wind was almost imperceptible, it was sufficient to wrench it about so that at first nothing could be done, and when steam was gotten up, the burning alcohol blew about so as to seriously injure the inflammable parts. Finally, the engines being under full steam, the launch was attempted, but, owing to the difficulties alluded to and to a failure in the construction of the launching piece, the aerodrome was thrown down upon the boat, fortunately with little damage.

Whatever form of launch was used it became evident at this time that the aerodrome must at any rate be firmly held, up to the very instant of release, and a device was arranged for clamping it to the launching apparatus.

On November 24th another attempt was made to launch, which was rendered impossible by a very moderate wind indeed.

On November 27th a new apparatus was arranged to merely drop the aerodrome over the water, with the hope that it would get up sufficient speed before reaching the surface to soar, but it was found that a very gentle intermittent breeze (probably not more than three or four miles an hour) was sufficient to make it impossible even to prepare to *drop* the aerodrome toward the water with safety.

It is difficult to give an idea in few words of the nature of the trouble, but unless one stands with the machine in the open air he can form no conception of what the difficulties are which are peculiar to practice in the open, and which do not present themselves to the constructor in the shop, nor probably to the mind of the reader.

December 1st, another failure; December 7th, another; December 11th, another; December 20th, another; December 21st, another. These do not all involve a separate journey, but five separate trips were made of a round distance of 60 miles each before the close of the season. It may be remembered that these attempts were in a site far from the conveniences of the workshop, and under circumstances which took up a great deal of time, for some hours were spent on mounting the aerodrome on each occasion, and the year closed without a single cast of it into the air. It was not known how it would have behaved there, for there had not been a launch, even, in nine trials, each one representing an amount of trouble and difficulty which this narrative gives no adequate idea of.

I pass over a long period of subsequent baffled effort, with the statement that numerous devices for launching were tried in vain, and that nearly a year passed before one was effected.

Six trips and trials were made in the first six months of 1894, without securing a launch. On the 24th of October a new launching piece was tried for the first time, which embodied all the requisites whose necessity was taught by previous experience, and, saving occasional accidents, the launching was from this time forward accomplished with comparatively little difficulty.

The aerodromes were now for the first time put fairly in the air, and a new class of difficulties arose, due to a cause which was at first obscure, — for two successive launches of the same aerodrome, under conditions as near alike as possible, would be followed by entirely different results.   For example, in the first case it might be found rushing, not falling, forward and downward into the water under the impulse of its own engines; in the second case, with every condition from observation apparently the same, it might be found soaring upward until its wings made an angle of 60 degrees with the horizon, and, unable to sustain itself at such a slope, sliding backward into the water.

After much embarrassment the trouble was discovered to be due to the fact that the wings, though originally set at precisely the same position and same angle in the two cases, were irregularly deflected by the upward pressure of the air, so that they no longer had the form which they appeared to possess but a moment before they were upborne by it, and so that a very minute difference, too small to be certainly noted, exaggerated by this pressure, might cause the wind of advance to strike either below or above the wing and to produce the salient difference alluded to.   When this was noticed all aerodromes were inverted, and sand was dredged uniformly over the wings until its weight represented that of the machine.   The flexure of the wings under these circumstances must be nearly that in free air, and it was found to distort them beyond all anticipation. Here commences another series of trials in which the wings were strengthened in various ways, but in none of which, without incurring a prohibitive weight, was it possible to make them strong enough.   Various methods of guying them were tried, and they were rebuilt on different designs, — a slow and expensive process.   Finally, it may be said, in anticipation (and largely through the skill of Mr. Reed, the foreman of the work), the wings were rendered strong enough without excessive weight, but a year or more passed in these and other experiments.

In the latter part of 1894 two steel aerodromes had already been built which sustained from 40 to 50 per cent. of their dead-lift weight on the pendulum, and each of which was apparently supplied with much more than sufficient power for horizontal flight (the engine and all the moving parts furnishing over one-horse power at the brake weighed in one of these but 26 ounces); but it may be remarked that the boilers and engines in lifting this per cent. of the weight did so only at the best performance in the shop, and that nothing like this could be counted upon for regular performance in the open. Every experiment with the launch, when the aerodrome descended into the water, not gently, but impelled by the misdirected power of its own engines, resulted at this stage in severe strains and local injury, so that repairing, which was almost rebuilding, constantly went on, — a hard but necessary condition attendant on the necessity of trial in the free air. It was gradually found that it was indispensable to make the frame stronger than had hitherto been done, though the absolute limit of strength consistent with weight seemed to have been already reached, and the year 1895 was chiefly devoted to the labor on the wings and what seemed at first the hopeless task of improving the construction so that it might be stronger without additional weight, when every gramme of weight had already been scrupulously economized. With this went on attempts to carry the effective power of the burners, boilers, and engines further, and modification of the internal arrangement and a general disposition of the parts such that the wings could be placed further forward or backward at pleasure, to more readily meet the conditions necessary for bringing the centre of gravity under the centre of pressure. So little had even now been learned about the system of balancing in the open air that at this late day recourse was again had to rubber models, of a different character, however, from those previously used, for in the latter the rubber was strained, not twisted. These experiments took up an inordinate time, though the flight obtained from the models thus made was somewhat longer and much steadier than that obtained with the Penaud form, and from them a good deal of valuable information was gained as to the number and position of the wings, and as to the effectiveness of different forms and dispositions of them. By the middle of the year a launch took place with a brief flight, where the aerodrome shot down into the water after a little over 50 yards. It was immediately followed by one in which the same aerodrome rose at a considerable incline and fell backward, with scarcely any advance after sustaining itself rather less than ten seconds, and these and subsequent attempts showed that the problem of disposing of the wings so that they would not yield, and of obtaining a proper " balance," was not yet solved.

Briefly it may be said that the year 1895 gave small results for the labor with which it was filled, and that at its close the outlook for further substantial improvement seemed to be almost hopeless, but it was at this time that final success was drawing near. Shortly after its close I became convinced that substantial rigidity had been secured for the wings; that the frame had been made stronger without prohibitive weight, and that a degree of accuracy in the balance had been obtained which had not been hoped for. Still there had been such a long succession of disasters and accidents in the launching that hope was low when success finally came.

I have not spoken here of the aid which I received from others, and particularly from Doctor Carl Barus and Mr. J. E. Watkins, who have been at different times associated with me in the work. Mr. R. L. Reed's mechanical skill has helped me everywhere, and the lightness and efficiency of the engines are in a large part due to Mr. L. C. Maltby.

# THE AERODROMES IN FLIGHT.

THE successful flights of Dr. Langley's aerodrome were witnessed by Dr. Bell and described by him as follows: [1]

Through the courtesy of Dr. S. P. Langley, Secretary of the Smithsonian Institution, I have had, on various occasions, the privilege of witnessing his experiments with aerodromes, and especially the remarkable success attained by him in experiments made upon the Potomac river on Wednesday, May 6, 1896, which led me to urge him to make public some of these results.

I had the pleasure of witnessing the successful flight of some of these aerodromes more than a year ago, but Dr. Langley's reluctance to make the results public at that time prevented me from asking him, as I have done since, to let me give an account of what I saw.

On the date named two ascensions were made by the aerodrome, or so-called "flying-machine," which I will not describe here further than to say that it appeared to me to be built almost entirely of metal, and driven by a steam-engine which I have understood was carrying fuel and a water supply for a very brief period, and which was of extraordinary lightness.

The absolute weight of the aerodrome, including that of the engine and all appurtenances, was, as I was told, about 25 pounds, and the distance from tip to tip of the supporting surfaces was, as I observed, about 12 or 14 feet. The method of propulsion was by aerial screw-propellers, and there was no gas or other aid for lifting it in the air except its own internal energy.

On the occasion referred to, the aerodrome, at a given signal, started from a platform about 20 feet above the water, and rose at first directly in the face of the wind, moving at all times with remarkable steadiness, and subsequently swinging around in large curves of, perhaps, a hundred yards in diameter, and continually ascending until its steam was exhausted, when, at a lapse of about a minute and a half, and at a height which I

---

[1] " Nature," London, May 28, 1896.

(26)

Plate II.

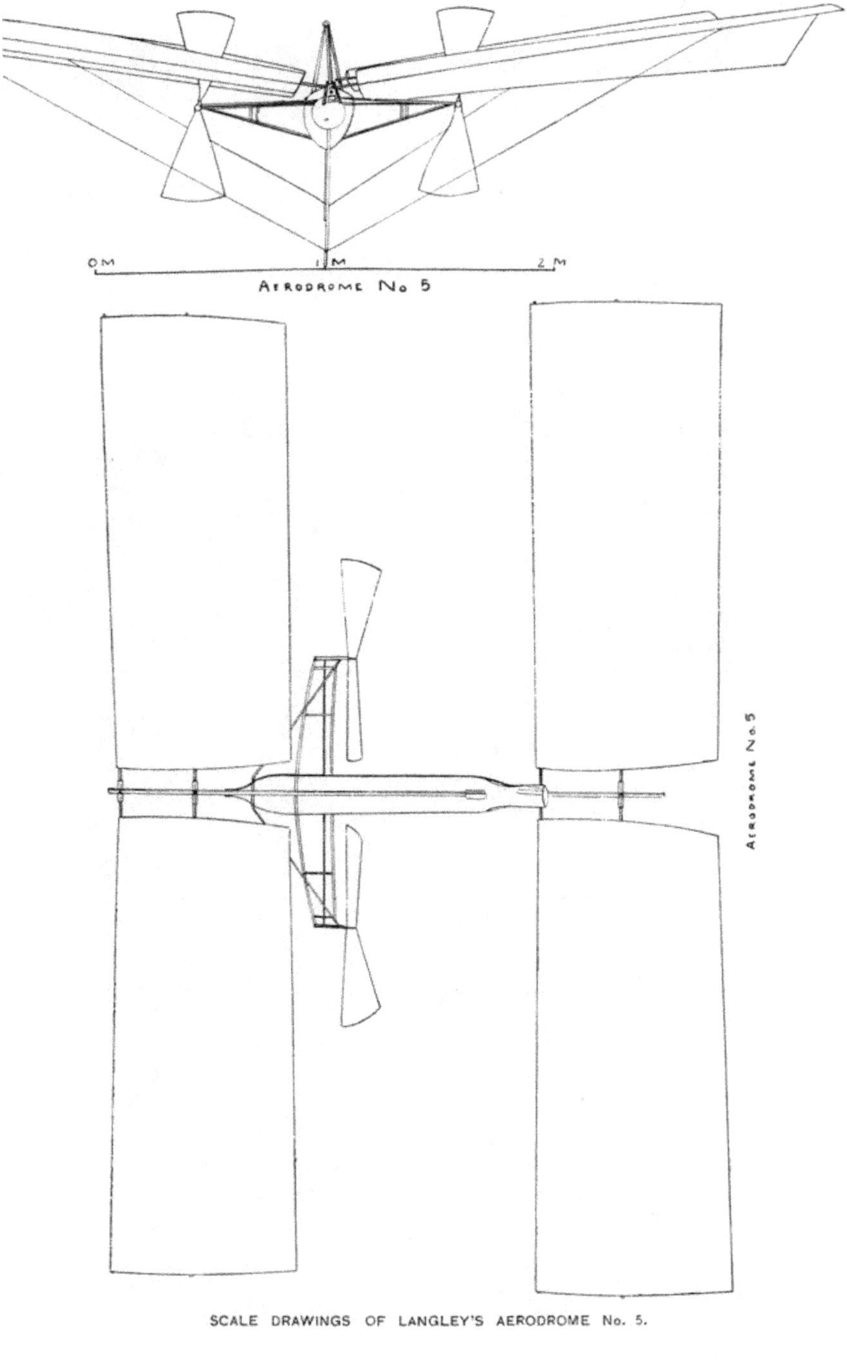

AERODROME No 5

AERODROME No. 5

SCALE DRAWINGS OF LANGLEY'S AERODROME No. 5.

Intentionally blank as was the original edition.

judged to be between 80 and 100 feet in the air, the wheels ceased turning, and the machine, deprived of the aid of its propellers, to my surprise did not fall, but settled down so softly and gently that it touched the water without the least shock, and was in fact immediately ready for another trial.

In the second trial, which followed directly, it repeated in nearly every respect the actions of the first, except that the direction of its course was different. It ascended again in the face of the wind, afterwards moving steadily and continually in large curves accompanied with a rising motion and a lateral advance. Its motion was, in fact, so steady, that I think a glass of water on its surface would have remained unspilled. When the steam gave out again, it repeated for a second time the experience of the first trial when the steam had ceased, and settled gently and easily down. What height it reached at this trial I cannot say, as I was not so favorably placed as in the first; but I had occasion to notice that this time its course took it over a wooded promontory, and I was relieved of some apprehension in seeing that it was already so high as to pass the tree-tops by 20 or 30 feet. It reached the water 1 minute and 31 seconds from the time it started, at a measured distance of over 900 feet from the point at which it rose.

This, however, was by no means the length of its flight. I estimated from the diameter of the curve described, from the number of turns of the propellers as given by the automatic counter, after due allowance for slip, and from other measures, that the actual length of flight on each occasion was slightly over 3,000 feet. It is at least safe to say that each exceeded half an English mile.

From the time and distance it will be noticed that the velocity was between 20 and 25 miles an hour, in a course which was taking it constantly "up hill." I may add that on a previous occasion I have seen a far higher velocity attained by the same aerodrome when its course was horizontal.

I have no desire to enter into detail further than I have done, but I cannot but add that it seems to me that no one who was present on this interesting occasion could have failed to recognize that the practicability of mechanical flight had been demonstrated.

ALEXANDER GRAHAM BELL.

Not long after the May experiments Dr. Langley went abroad for needed rest and recreation, and in the autumn, after his return, further experiments were tried.   On the 28th of November a flight was made which was more than three-quarters of a mile in length, the time occupied being precisely one minute and three-quarters.   Mr. Frank G. Carpenter was a fortunate witness of this, the longest flight ever made, and with Dr. Langley's approval he wrote a detailed account of it for the " Washington Star" of Dec. 12, 1896.   His article is interesting from beginning to end.

*Plate III.*

LANGLEY'S AERODROME IN FLIGHT.

May 6, 1896.

Intentionally blank as was the original edition.

# AERODROME No. 5, '96.

DR. LANGLEY has two successful aerodromes, No. 5 and No. 6; the former made the flights of May 6th and the latter that of November 28th. Plate II. gives scale drawings of No. 5, and Plate III. shows a perspective view of the same in flight. The weight of this, with fuel and water sufficient for the flights described, is about 30 pounds. The weight of the engine and boiler together is about 7 pounds. The power of the engine under full steam is rather more than one-horse power. There are two cylinders, each having a diameter of 1¼ inches. The piston stroke is 2 inches. The two screws are 39 inches from tip to tip, and are made to revolve in opposite directions; the pitch is 1¼; they are connected to the engines by bevel gears most carefully made; the shafts and gears are so arranged that the synchronous movement of the two screws is secured. The boiler is a coil of copper tubing; the diameter of the coil externally is 3 inches; the diameter of the tubing externally is ⅜ inch; the pressure of steam when the aerodrome is in flight varies from 110 to 150 pounds to the square inch. The flame is produced by the ælopile, which is a modification of the naphtha " blow-torch " used by plumbers; the heat of this flame is about 2,000 degrees Fahrenheit. Four pounds of water are carried at starting, and about ten ounces of naphtha. In action the boiler evaporates about one pound of water per minute. Flights could be greatly lengthened by adding a condenser and using the water over and over again, but, as Dr. Langley says, the time for that will come later.

(29)

# RECENT EXPERIMENTS IN GLIDING FLIGHT.

By O. Chanute.

Having for a number of years studied the physical principles underlying flight, and having passed in review the experiments of others in a series of articles which eventually swelled into a book,[1] I ultimately reached the conclusion that the contingent compassing of artificial flight by man involved the study of at least ten separate problems, or the devising of means for observing and mastering the conditions enumerated as follows:

1. The resistance and supporting power of air.
2. The motor, its character and its energy.
3. The instrument for obtaining propulsion.
4. The form and kind of the apparatus.
5. The extent of the sustaining surfaces.
6. The material and texture of the apparatus.
7. The maintenance of the equilibrium.
8. The guidance in any desired direction.
9. The starting up under all conditions.
10. The alighting safely anywhere.

It is probable that some of these problems can be solved in more ways than one, and these solutions must then be harmoniously combined in a design which shall deal with the general problem as a whole, before the best possible result is attained.

I further reached the conclusion that the seventh problem, the maintenance of the equilibrium under all circumstances, was by far the most important, and the first which should be solved; that until automatic stability, at all angles of flight and conditions of wind, was evolved, and safety thereby secured, it

---

[1] "Progress in the Flying Machines," M. N. Forney, N.Y., Editor, 1894.

would be premature to seek to apply a motor or a propelling instrument in a full-sized machine, as these additions would introduce complications which might be avoided at the beginning.

I seriously doubted, at first, whether automatic stability could be secured with an artificial machine; whether such combinations could be devised, for an inanimate apparatus, as to perform the complicated functions of the life and instinct of the birds, who probably preserve their balance through almost unconscious reflex action of their nerves and muscles. Observation, however, indicated that this might be automatic, requiring no thought under ordinary conditions, and the final conclusion was reached that it might be possible to evolve an artificial apparatus which should afford automatic stability and safety most of the time; that the variations of the wind were the great difficulties to be encountered, that they must be met and overcome, and that perhaps they might be utilized in obtaining propulsion and support, as is daily done by the soaring birds.

I therefore published an article in the "Engineering Magazine" for April, 1896, in which I advised those seeking a solution of the problem of flight to turn their attention to experiments in soaring flight, with full-sized apparatus carrying a man, as the quickest, cheapest, and surest way of ascertaining the exact conditions which must be met in practical flight.

This mode of procedure doubtless involves a certain amount of personal danger of accident. It might be pointed out that the advice is easy to give, but hazardous to follow, and so I further determined to try such experiments myself, so far as my limited personal means would allow.

For this purpose I secured the services of Mr. A. M. Herring, who had tried some experiments of his own. He rebuilt for me his Lilienthal apparatus, with which he had made some gliding flights in 1894, and he also built another full-sized gliding apparatus after a design of my own.

These were completed in June, 1896, and on the 22d of that month we, a party of four persons, went into camp in the desert sand hills on the south shore of Lake Michigan, just north of the station of Miller, Ind., 30 miles east of Chicago.

These sand hills have been piled up by the wind blowing the sand from the beach. They gradually increase in altitude, from a point about 10 miles east of Chicago to the vicinity of St. Joseph, Mich., on the east shore of the lake, where they attain a height of 200 or 300 feet. They occupy a strip two to five miles wide around the south and south-eastern turns of Lake Michigan, and are bleak, bare, and deserted, being entirely incapable of cultivation. North of Miller, Ind., these hills rise about 70 feet above the lake. They are of soft yellow sand, almost bare of vegetation, and face in every direction of the compass, so that almost all directions of wind can be utilized in gliding experiments.

The method of carrying on these adventures is for the operator to place himself within and under the apparatus, which should, preferably, be light enough to be easily carried on the shoulders or by the hands, and to face the wind on a hillside. The operator should in no wise be attached to the machine. He may be suspended by his arms, or sit upon a seat, or stand on a dependent running board, but he must be able to disengage himself instantly from the machine should anything go wrong, and be able to come down upon his legs in landing.

Facing dead into the wind, and keeping the front edge of the supporting surfaces depressed, so that the wind shall blow upon their backs and press them downward, the operator first adjusts his apparatus and himself to the veering wind. He has to struggle to obtain a poise, and in a moment of relative steadiness he runs forward a few steps as fast as he may, and launches himself upon the breeze, by raising up the front edge of the sustaining surfaces, so as to receive the wind from beneath at a very small angle (2 to 4 degrees) of incidence. If the surfaces and wind be adequate, he finds himself thoroughly sustained, and then sails forward on a descending or undulating course, under the combined effects of gravity and of the opposing wind. By shifting either his body or his wings, or both, he can direct his descent, either sideways or up or down, within certain limits;

he can cause the apparatus to sweep upward so as to clear an obstacle, and he is not infrequently lifted up several feet by a swelling of the wind. The course of the glide eventually brings the apparatus within a few feet of the ground (6 to 10 feet), when the operator, by throwing his weight backward, or his wings forward if they be movable, causes the front of the supporting surfaces to tilt up to a greater angle of incidence, thus increasing the wind resistance, slowing the forward motion, and enabling him, by a slight oscillation, to drop to the ground as gently as if he had fallen only one or two feet.

These manœuvres require considerable quickness and dexterity, yet they are easily learned in a few days, the principal rule to be learned being that the movements to be bodily made are the reverse of those instinctive motions which would occur to catch one's self from falling if walking on the ground. In point of fact, we found that a week's practice sufficed for a young, active man to become reasonably expert in these manœuvres, and hundreds of glides were made with the several machines, experimented in 1896 under variable conditions of wind, without the slightest personal accident.

As before stated, we went into camp on the 22d of June, 1896. The party consisted of Mr. A. M. Herring, already mentioned, Mr. W. Avery, an electrician and carpenter, Mr. William Paul Butusov, a former sailor, and myself. The tent was large enough to shelter the machines, but we learned in a few days that this precaution was unnecessary, and that they could be safely left exposed to the wind, outside, by tying them down to pegs or to bushes, or even by loading them down with sand. There was a fishing station of two houses within a mile of the tent, from which outside aid might have been obtained in the improbable case of an accident. Miller Station was two miles inland, and, having come through that station with our suspicious baggage, we soon had more visitors than was altogether pleasant in preliminary experiments.

The Lilienthal machine was first set up. It is shown, poised for a flight, in Plate IV., Fig. 1. The wings were 20 feet from tip to tip, 7 feet 6 inches in maximum breadth, and measured

168 square feet in surface, with a weight of 36 pounds. Mr. Herring, who had used it before, took the lead in gliding with it.

It was realized from the first that the machine was difficult to handle and to poise in the wind. The variable puffs pelted the apparatus; they occasionally lifted one wing more than the other, or rocked the machine fore and aft, so that a struggle was necessary before a poise could be obtained. Once under way the same action continued, and the operator was compelled to shift his weight constantly, like a tight-rope dancer without a pole, in order to bring the centre of gravity directly under the centre of pressure and to avoid being upset. This, in fact, is the principle of the Lilienthal apparatus. The equilibrium depends upon the constant readjustment of the weight, so as to coincide with the variable position of the centre of pressure due to the shifting direction and force of the wind. Lilienthal, who evolved this machine, so superior to any that had preceded it, was an expert in its use. He made thousands of flights without serious accident; but it is due to those who may desire to repeat such experiments to state here plainly that we found it cranky and uncertain in its action and requiring great prac- tice. If strongly built it was not, however, nearly so hazardous to life and limb as the above statement would seem to imply. The radiating ribs forming the frame of the wings extend down- ward about as low as the waist of the operator when in flight, and whenever an awkward landing is made, by reason of the apparatus tilting to one side or the other, the ribs on that side are the first to strike the ground. Acting as springs, breaking or not as the case might be, they save the operator from bodily harm even in a descent of 20 feet. These breakages were easily repaired by wiring on wooden splints to the ribs, so that practice could be resumed in a few minutes.

About 100 glides were made with this machine, the longest being 116 feet, and the heights started from were 20 to 30 feet in winds of 12 to 17 miles per hour. Mr. Avery proved an apt pupil, and in the course of a week learned to manage the machine nearly as well as Mr. Herring. Mr. Butusov did not do so well and was upset, but not harmed. I did not venture

*Plate IV.*

Fig. I. — GLIDING MACHINE.    p. 33.

Fig. 2. — See p. 35.

Intentionally blank as was the original edition.

myself, feeling that I was no longer young and active enough to perform such acrobatic exercises without breaking the apparatus. After it had been broken, mended, tried again, and overhauled a goodly number of times, it was finally decided, on the 29th of June, to discard it, and it was accordingly broken up.

This decision was most unfortunately justified on the 10th of the succeeding August, when Herr Lilienthal met his death while experimenting with a machine based on the same principle, but with two superposed sets of wings. This deplorable accident removed the man who has hitherto done most to show that human flight is probably possible, who was the first in modern times to endeavor to imitate the soaring birds with full-sized apparatus, and who was so well equipped in every way that he probably would have accomplished final success if he had lived.

Having discarded the Lilienthal machine, we next turned our attention to the apparatus after my own design. This was based upon just the reverse of the principle involved in the Lilienthal apparatus.[1] Instead of the man moving about, to bring the centre of gravity under the centre of pressure, it was intended that the wings should move automatically so as to bring the movable centre of pressure back over the centre of gravity, which latter should remain fixed. That is to say, that the wings should move instead of the man.

The apparatus consisted in 12 wings, each 6 feet long by 3 feet wide, measuring $14\frac{3}{4}$ square feet in area, each pivoted at its root to a central frame, so that it could move fore and aft, this action being restrained by springs. The main frame was so constructed that the wings could be grouped in various ways, so as to ascertain the best arrangement for maximum support and for counterbalancing the effects of wind gusts, if possible. The total wing surface was 177 square feet, and the weight was 37 pounds. Fig. 2, Plate IV., shows the first grouping tested, which was found at once to be reasonably steady, but deficient in lifting power. It was recognized that the wings interfered

---

[1] To establish priority of invention a patent has been applied for.

with each other's efficiency; that the wind was deflected downward by the front wings, so that the middle and rear wings did not afford the same sustaining power as at the front. After making a few glides with this arrangement, a series of changes was tried to ascertain what was the best grouping and the best distance between the wings in order to obtain the maximum lift and the greatest steadiness. The paths of the wind currents in each arrangement of the wings were indicated by liberating bits of down in front of the machine, and, under their guidance, six permutations were made, each of which was found to produce an improvement in actual gliding flight over its predecessors.

The final arrangement to which this series of experiments led is shown on page 53. Five of the pairs of wings had gradually accumulated at the front, and the operator was directly under them, while the sixth pair of wings formed a tail at the rear, and being mounted so as to flex upward behind in flight, preserved the fore and aft balance. It was at once demonstrated that this apparatus was steady, safe, and manageable in winds up to 20 miles an hour. With it about 100 glides were made. The longest of these was 82 feet, in a descending course of about 1 in 4, against a wind of 13 miles an hour; the object constantly in view being not to make long glides, but to study the equilibrium of the machine and the principles which should govern in developing it further. These were found to be that the supporting surfaces should be concentrated at the front and the man placed directly under them; that the lowest wings should be at least $2\frac{1}{2}$ feet above the ground; that they should be about two-thirds of their breadth apart vertically, and not less than their breadth apart horizontally, being set so as to present an angle of incidence of 3 to 7 degrees above the horizon when in flight, and that the wings should be pivoted so as to move very easily, the friction upon this first set of pivots having been found entirely too great to permit the wings adjusting themselves easily to the variations of the wind, and the man having had to move his body.

Having ascertained these facts, the experiments were termi-

Plate V.

CHANUTE'S 1896 GLIDING MACHINE IN FLIGHT.

Working drawings of this machine are given in Plate VII. Another view of the same machine is shown in Fig. I, Plate VI.

Intentionally blank as was the original edition.

nated on the 4th of July, and the equipment was sent back to Chicago in order to rebuild the machine.

It may safely be asserted that more was learned concerning the practical requirements of flight during the two weeks occupied by these experiments than I had gathered during many previous years of study of the principles involved, and of experiments with models. The latter are instructive, it is true, but they do not reveal all the causes for the vicissitudes which occur in the wind. They do not explain why models seldom pursue exactly the same course, why they swerve to the right or left, why they oscillate, or why they upset. When a man is riding on a machine, however, and his safety depends upon the observance of all the conditions, he keenly heeds what is happening to him, and he gets entirely new and more accurate conceptions of the character of the element which he is seeking to master.

The fact which most strongly impressed itself upon us was the inconstancy of the wind. It is incessantly changing in direction and in strength. This fact is not new, it has been well shown experimentally by Mr. A. F. Zahm, by Professor Langley, and probably by others, but its effects upon a man-ridden machine must be seen and felt to realize that this is the great obstacle to be overcome in compassing artificial flight. It cannot be avoided, it cannot be temporized with, and it must be coped with and conquered before we can hope to have a practical flying-machine.

One remarkable feature of the wind, however, struck us as hitherto unknown, or at least unmentioned. *The wind gusts seem to come in as rolling waves*, rotating at a higher speed than the general forward movement. The buffetings which the apparatus received from the wind, while the operator was endeavoring to steady it, preparatory to a flight, seemed to indicate that he was struggling with a rotary billow which produced the fluctuations. Professor Langley has termed these fluctuations " the internal work of the wind," and it is quite conceivable that they should be produced by a revolving motion, striking the surfaces with velocities varying with the distance from the centre of rotation, and producing all the pulsations which have been revealed by the instrumental measurements.

Mr. Herring first called my attention to this feature of the wind, and I have ever since been wondering how I could, for so many years, have been watching smoke curling away from chimneys, steam convolving from trains, or dust and leaves whirling in wind gusts, without realizing that the elastic tenuity of air must perforce produce rotary motions much more active than those which occur in water.

This observation, if confirmed by further investigation, promises to give us a better understanding of the forces to be mastered. There are indications that there is a certain synchronism about these air waves, and that arrangements can be devised, not only to encounter them, but to avail of them in securing propulsion and automatic stability.

Be this as it may, we returned to Chicago much encouraged by the result of these preliminary experiments, with much clearer ideas as to the difficulties to be surmounted, and with good hopes that by reconstructing the machine we could obtain still better performances.

The original twelve-winged machine was reconstructed by pivoting the wings upon ball-bearings placed at the top and bottom of wooden uprights fastened to the main frame. The wings at the front were reduced to ten in number, in order to space them further apart without increasing their total height, but one pair was soon taken off, and the required supporting surface was restored by placing a concave aeroplane over the top of the wings. Two pairs of wings, superposed, were placed at the rear, but one pair was taken off after the first few trials, and the apparatus, provided with a rear keel or rudder, assumed the shape shown in Plate VI., Fig. 1. The total supporting surface at the front was then 143.5 square feet, the wings at the back measured 29.5 square feet, and the weight was 33½ pounds. The ball-bearings are at the level of the lower and of the third pair of wings from the bottom in the figure, and each set of moving wings, four in number, is connected rigidly by vertical wooden rods and diagonal wire ties so as to move

*Plate VI.*

Fig. I. — CHANUTE'S 1896 GLIDING MACHINE.   p. 38.

Fig. 2. — CHANUTE'S TWO-SURFACE GLIDING MACHINE.   p. 39.

Intentionally blank as was the original edition.

together.   Elastic rubber springs at front and rear connect them with the frame and restrain the movements produced by the fluctuations of the wind and relative speed.   The detailed construction of the apparatus is shown on Plate VII.   It had been originally intended to erect the machine with five pairs of superposed wings at the front, and they were in fact put on, but the first few trials in the wind showed that the height and leverage were too great for easy control, and the top pair was accordingly taken off.

There was built simultaneously another full-sized machine, based upon a different principle.   Instead of having pivoted wings, this consisted of three superposed concave surfaces, stretching 16 feet across the line of motion, by a breadth of 4 feet 3 inches, these surfaces measuring an aggregate of 191 square feet.   The lower surface was cut away at the centre to admit the body of the operator.   The machine was provided with a combined horizontal and vertical rudder, and its total weight was 31 pounds.   The first few trials developed the fact that the sustaining power was in excess, and that the bottom surface was too near the ground.   It was removed, leaving the apparatus in the condition shown on Plate VI., Fig. 2.   The sustaining surfaces and the rudder were connected by an automatic device, designed by Mr. Herring, for the purpose of securing stability.   The curvature of the wings (versed sine) was about one-tenth of the chord.   Estimates were made in advance of head resistance due to the framing and to the drift of this machine.   It was computed that it required a relative speed of 22 miles an hour and an angle of incidence of 3 degrees for support, and that its angle of gliding descent would be 10 degrees, or 1 in 5.6, which computations were fully verified in the experiments, as will be seen hereafter.

Still a third full-sized machine was constructed at my expense at the same time.   This was designed by Mr. William Paul Butusov, who has already been mentioned as being present at the preliminary trials in June, and who stated that he had already tested with success a similar construction some seven years previously.   This closely resembled the apparatus experimented by Le Bris in 1855 and 1867. It consisted in a boat-like frame of ribs and stanchions, which might be covered with stout oil-cloth and thus transformed into a boat. Above this were four longitudinal keels of balloon cloth, stretched on a frame, each 8 feet long and 3 feet deep. The central space was left open, but the two side spaces were roofed over. This occupied 8 feet in width, and immediately above were placed the wings, each 16 feet long, by a maximum width of 7 feet, tapering to the tips. The total spread was, therefore, 40 feet from tip to tip, and above this again a square aeroplane or kite was placed, hung on trunnions at its centre, so that its angle of incidence might be varied at will by lines carried to the hands of the operator. The latter stood upright in the boat on a running board 8 feet long, and might therefore shift his weight to that extent by walking forward or backward, and he might also shift it about 3 feet sideways by leaning to one side or the other. The whole arrangement is shown in Plate VIII., Fig. 1, except the rudder and tail, which are partly hidden by the man, and which are moved by light lines passing over pulleys and carried to his hands. In addition to this a pair of parallel bars (curtain-poles) were fastened to the frame, to which the man might cling or brace himself.

When finally completed the apparatus spread 266 square feet of sustaining surface and weighed 160 pounds. The various parts (wings, keel-roofs, top aeroplane, and tail) were then tested by suspending them inverted, and loading them with sand to the maximum load they might be called upon to carry, and as some of them showed signs of crippling, or did cripple, they were strengthened with additional material until they were safe to stand the strains. This brought the total weight up to 190 pounds.

These three machines being ready, we again went to the sand hills on the 20th of August, 1896. Having on the previous occasion found the vicinity of Miller too accessible to the public, we went, this time, five miles further down the beach, where the hills were higher, the solitude greater, and the path more obscure to the railroad, which it reached at a sand-pit

Plate VII.

Plan,
*Viewed from top*

Scale
0   1   2   3   4 Feet

*Side Elevation.*

B

B

B          B

B          B

*Front Elevation.*

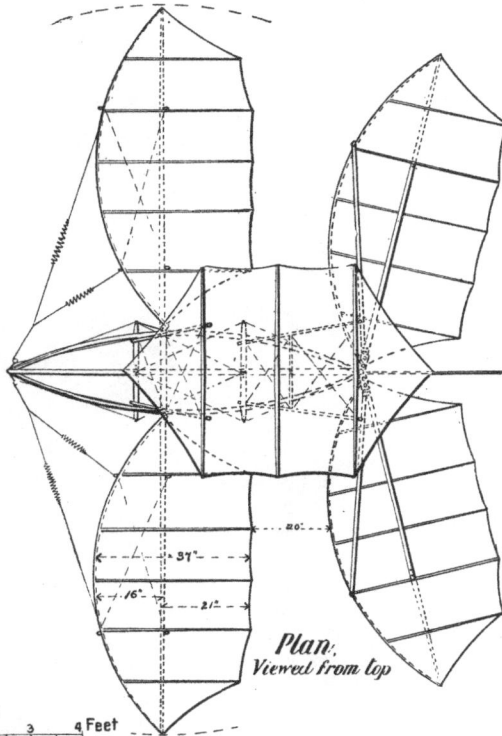

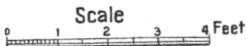

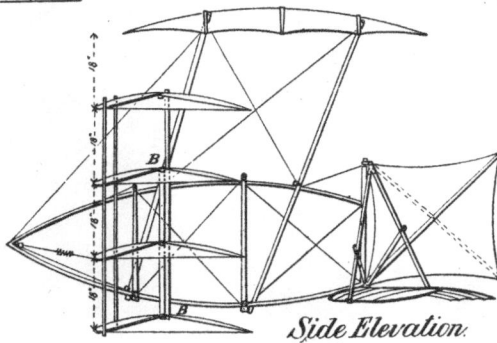

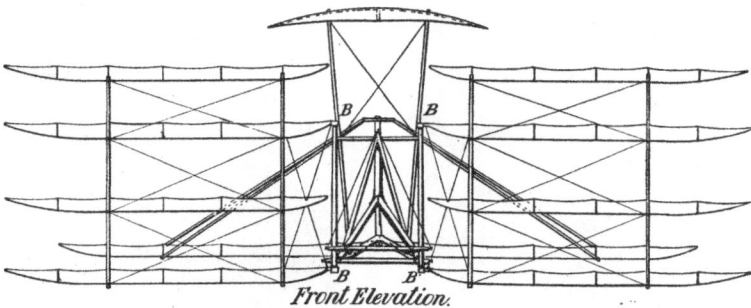

MULTIPLE-WING GLIDING MACHINE, Invented by O. CHANUTE, C.E.

Intentionally blank as was the original edition.

station consisting of a single house, and called Dune Park. The distance from our camp was about two miles, through a series of swamps, woods, and hills, so that intending visitors not infrequently got lost.

We went from Chicago by a sailing vessel in order to avoid arousing gossip at the railroad station, and in the afternoon of August 21st we got the material unloaded and the tent pitched at the experimental hill. We hoped to begin setting up the machines on the morrow.

Unfortunately, that very night a fearful storm and whirling wind came up from the south-west at 3 A.M. It blew the tent to ribbons, blew away and wrecked such wings as were not boxed, while all of the party and the provisions were drenched, the camp equipage being moreover scattered and damaged.[1] It became necessary to send at once to Chicago for another tent, which arrived at Dune Park by express in the afternoon of the twenty-second, but this disclosed our presence to the people at the sand pit, and some ten days later brought down the newspaper reporters to see what we were about.

Our party consisted of five persons, Mr. Herring, Mr. Avery, Mr. Butusov, already mentioned, Dr. Ricketts, — a young surgeon who found that function such an entire sinecure that he could only exhibit to us his talents in cooking,— and myself. In addition to this there was, for a time, a carpenter to erect the trestle work from which to launch the Butusov machine. The hill selected faced the north and rose 100 feet above the lake, there being an intervening beach of about 350 feet between its base and the water. It was of soft yellow sand with many bare slopes, but with occasional clumps of trees and bushes. To the south it sloped to a bare wilderness of sand.

The first machine which was repaired and set up after the tornado was the aerocurve, with three superposed fixed surfaces and automatic tail attachment. It was first tested on the 29th of August, with tentative glides from a height of 15 to 20 feet above the bottom of the hill, but it was found to rock so that the lower surface struck the ground, hard to manage, and to lift

---

[1] The frying-pan was blown 200 yards away.

more than required. The lower aerocurve was therefore taken off, thus reducing the sustaining surface to 135 square feet, and the weight to 23 pounds. This was thereafter found ample to sustain an aggregate weight of 178 pounds (23 pounds of machine and 155 pounds of operator), and all the subsequent experiments were made with this arrangement. During the next 14 days scores and scores of glides were made with this machine, whenever the wind served. It was found steady, easy to handle before starting, and under good control when under way, — a motion of the operator's body of not over 2 inches proving as effective as a motion of 5 or more inches in the Lilienthal machine. It was experimented in all sorts of winds, from 10 to 31 miles an hour, the latter being believed to be a higher wind than any gliding machine had been tried in theretofore, and yet the equilibrium was not compromised, the machine gliding steadily at speeds of about 17 miles per hour with reference to the ground, and of about 20 to 40 miles an hour with reference to the air, or relative wind. On one occasion a relative speed of 52 miles an hour was acquired in a descent. Some of the best glides made were as follows:

| Operator. | Length in feet. | Time in seconds. | Angle of descent. | Height fallen, feet. | Speed, feet per second. | Descent of |
|---|---|---|---|---|---|---|
| Avery.......... | 199 | 8. | 10° | 34.6 | 24.9 | 1 in 5.75 |
| Herring ........ | 234 | 8.7 | 7½° | 30.4 | 26.9 | 1 " 7.69 |
| Avery .......... | 253 | ......... | 10½° | 46. | ......... | 1 " 5.50 |
| Herring ........ | 239 | ......... | 11° | 46.3 | ......... | 1 " 5.24 |
| " ........ | 220 | 9. | ......... | ......... | 24.4 | |
| " ........ | 235 | 10.3 | ......... | ......... | 22.8 | |
| Avery .......... | 256 | 10.2 | 8° | 25.5 | 25.1 | 1 in 7.18 |
| Herring ........ | 359 | 14. | 10° | 62.1 | 25.6 | 1 " 5.75 |

One of these flights is shown by Fig. 2, Plate VIII.

The varying flatness of the angle of descent was undoubtedly due to the varying strength of the wind, and also to its ascend-

*Plate VIII.*

Fig. 1. — See p. 40.

Fig. 2. — A GOOD START.

Intentionally blank as was the original edition.

ing trends as it struck the slope of the hill.   The latter were exhibited by liberating bits of down at the foot of the hill, whence they would ascend parallel with the surface and pass over the top to the plain beyond.   On many occasions the machine and man were raised higher than the starting point by increasing wind velocity, but this action was found to be much too irregular to be availed of as a source of power.

It was found that by moving the operator's body backward or forward, an undulatory course could be imparted to the apparatus.   It could be made to rise several feet to clear an obstacle, or the flight might be prolonged, when approaching the ground, by causing the machine to rise somewhat steeply and then continuing the glide at a flatter angle.  It was very interesting to see the aviator on the hillside adjust his machine and himself to the veering wind, then, when poised, take a few running steps forward, sometimes but one step, and raising slightly the front of his apparatus, sail off at once horizontally against the wind; to see him pass with steady motion and ample support 40 or 50 feet above the observer, and then, having struck the zone of comparative calm produced by eddies from the hill, gradually descend to land on the beach several hundred feet away.

A few hidden defects were gradually evolved, such as lack of adjustment in the automatic device, and occasional swerving out of the course in sudden gusts of wind; but safe landings were made in every case, by simply throwing the body back and causing the front edge of the aerocurve to rise so as to diminish the speed; and the machine was not once broken. It was kept out of doors moored to pegs driven in the sand, and was injured by storms on but three occasions.   It was concluded, however; that a permanent machine of this kind should be arranged to fold up (as this was not) so as to admit of carrying it about and of sheltering it from the weather.

The movable winged machine (12 wings) was not set up till the 4th of September, 1896.   Upon being tested, it was found at once that a mistake had been made in not providing entirely new wings for it.   The old wings were so racked, twisted, and distorted by their prior service that they did not lift alike, and that it was difficult to poise the machine and to balance it in the wind. Nothing is so important in such experiments as to keep the sustaining surfaces in perfect shape and to prevent any racking when under strains. This is inculcated to us by the birds, who are constantly " pluming " themselves when on the perch. They pass each flying feather through their beaks, repair those barbs which have become separated, rearrange the lap of the feathers, and beat their wings up and down to limber up the muscles. I have reason to believe that it was in consequence of the failure to keep his apparatus in constant rigid good order that Herr Lilienthal so unhappily lost his life. A correspondent in Germany, who had witnessed his exercises two weeks before the fatal fall, wrote me that he had found that in the particular machine with which the accident occurred " the connections of the wings and of the steering arrangements were very bad and unreliable," that he had remonstrated with Herr Lilienthal very seriously, and the latter had promised that he would put the apparatus in order, but, with that contempt of danger which long familiarity and thousands of successful flights is sure to create, it is much to be feared that he did not attend to it immediately, especially as he was about to discard that particular machine for a new one from which he expected great results.

It was also found that in spacing the wings of the twelve-winged machine further apart, it had been made too high. The top was 10 feet 6 inches above the ground, and the leverage of the wind made it difficult for the operator to control the machine. The top pair of wings was accordingly taken off, and the experiments thereafter made with the apparatus as cut down. In this shape it proved steady and manageable, the flights being over twice as long, with the same fall as with the original machine in June. The following are some of the glides made on the 11th of September against a wind of 22.3 miles per hour:

| Operator. | Length in feet. | Time in seconds. | Speed, feet per second. | Remarks. |
|---|---|---|---|---|
| Herring .......... | 148 | 7. | 21.1 | Angle not measured. |
| Avery ............ | 174 | 7.6 | 22.9 | " " " |
| Herring .......... | 166 | 7.5 | 22.1 | " " " |
| Avery ............ | 183 | 7.9 | 23.1 | " " " |
| Herring .......... | 172 | 7.8 | 22. | " " " |

The angles were approximately 10 or 11 degrees, or 1 in 5.

This machine had been provided with a swinging seat, consisting of network with a narrow board at its front, and with a pair of swinging bars and stirrups against which the legs could be braced, so as to move the wings fore and aft by means of light lines running through pulleys. The heights started from being only 30 to 35 feet above the base of the hill, and the glides being accordingly very brief, these attachments could not be brought into action, but their efficacy was tested by suspending the apparatus between two trees and facing the wind with a man in the seat. It was found, as was expected, that by thrusting the wings forward the machine was tossed up, and *vice versa* that by thrusting one wing forward the machine turned towards the opposite side, and that these would be effective ways of directing the apparatus when under flight, either up or down, or in a circling sweep. The automatic regulation, however, did not work as well as was hoped, perhaps in consequence of inaccurate adjustment of the springs. The man still had to move about one inch to preserve the equilibrium when under way. The machine made steady flights and easy landings, and was not once broken in action. It is certainly considered safer and more manageable than the Lilienthal apparatus which we tested. No photographs were taken of this machine in flight, as it was not tested nearly so often as would have been desirable, and whenever it was, something always interfered to prevent getting the camera.

It must be confessed that the results with this apparatus were rather disappointing, and yet the principle is believed to be sound.   As the variations of the wind are constantly changing the position of the centre of pressure, it is necessary that either the wings or the weight shall move, or that the angle of incidence relative to the air shall be absolutely maintained in order to keep the centre of pressure and the centre of gravity upon the same vertical line.   These are the two principles which are involved in the two machines which have herein been described. Which of the two shall hereafter prove to be most effective in practical use, or whether the two can be combined, cannot be determined at present, but it is my judgment that one or two more seasons should be devoted to perfecting the automatic equilibrium, to eliminating hidden defects, and to adjusting the strength of the springs and moving parts, before it will be prudent to apply a motor, or to try to imitate the soaring of the sailing birds.

Towards the last we gathered such confidence in the safety of the machines that we allowed anybody to try them who wanted to. A number of amateurs took short flights, awkwardly of course, but safely.   One of them was raised about 40 feet vertically and came down again so gently that he felt no jar upon alighting.   Others glided from 70 to 150 feet, and all agreed that the sensation of coasting on the air was delightful, although they were somewhat timid about tempting fate too many times. Any young, active man can become expert in a week with either of these machines.

We performed nothing like continuous soaring with any of the machines.   The fluctuations of the wind were entirely too irregular to be availed of; for a wind gust, which tossed a machine up, was almost immediately succeeded by a lull which let it down again.   If we had had a long, straight ridge, bare of trees at its summit, and a suitable wind blowing at right angles thereto, we would have attempted to have sailed horizontally along the top of the ridge, transversely to the resulting ascending current.   This manœuvre is frequently and easily performed by the soaring birds over the edge of a belt of trees.   They

ride across the face of the ascending aerial billow, decompos-
ing its upward trend into propulsion as well as support.    The
feat should be performable by man, and should, in my judgment, be attempted before circling flight is tried.    It requires,
of course, that the equilibrium shall be first mastered, and also
that the angle of flight shall be flatter than with our machines.
This was, as has been seen, from 8 degrees to 11 degrees, or a
descent of 1 in 7 or 1 in 5.    Now, the soaring birds generally
sail at angles of 4 degrees to 6 degrees, or a descent of 1 in
15 to 1 in 9, and hence they lose very much less elevation.
This disadvantage in the machines resulted from the increased
head resistance due to the framing and spars as compared
with the wing edges of the birds, and especially from the fact
that in order to give the man easy command over his movements and to let him land on his feet, he has to be in the natural
erect position.    This produces a body resistance due to about
5 square feet of surface, while it would be that due to only about
1 square foot if the man were placed horizontally, as is the body
of the bird.    It is probable, however, that the machines can be
improved in this respect, and that flatter angles of flight will be
obtained than those recorded herein.

The apparatus of Mr. Butusov, like that of Le Bris, had been
inspired by watching the sailing of the albatross in southern
latitudes.    He stated that having begun by experimenting with
the main wings, he had been led to add various adjuncts, such
as the keels and the top aeroplane in order to improve the stability.    It was no part of the original programme to test such a
machine, but in view of the degree of success said to have been
attained both by Le Bris and by Mr. Butusov, it was determined
to give the apparatus a trial.

As it weighed 190 pounds, and the operator's own weight
was 130 pounds, a total of 320 pounds, it was necessary to
furnish special appliances for launching the machine.    This was
provided for by building an inclined trestle work, which consisted in a pair of tallowed guides or ways, 8 feet apart, descending at an angle of 23 degrees down the slope of the sand
hill selected, the top being 94 feet and the bottom 67 feet above

the lake.   The last 10 feet of these launching ways was horizontal, and connected with the sloping portion by a curve of 5 feet radius.   The ways stood about 11 feet above the side of the hill, the central space between them being entirely unobstructed, the supports being braced by raking posts and braces. The trestle faced due north, so as to avail of the north wind, which, blowing down the whole length of Lake Michigan, arrived with fewer of the whirls and eddies than prevailed with the winds coming from the south,   south-east, or south-west. These had been disturbed by blowing over the sand hills, and it is a peculiarity well worthy of note by other experimenters that they will find it much preferable to avail of winds which have traversed across a sheet of water or a level plain than of those which have come over hills, trees, or other obstacles.

This fixed position of the launching ways, however, unfortunately required the waiting for a north wind to blow before experiments could be conducted with this apparatus.   The prevailing winds in September were from the south, and there were many storms, so that the instances were rare indeed, during the three weeks which elapsed after the trestle and apparatus were completed, when the wind came from the right direction, and with just the velocity (18 to 25 miles per hour) which was desired.   Hence the machine was not given that complete and thorough test which it would have received had the inventor accepted my proposal to launch from ways rigged up on a floating barge, which might have been anchored or towed against any wind of suitable velocity.

Before proceeding with the tests, the whole apparatus was carefully measured.   It was ascertained that the whole sectional area of the framing, spars, wing edges, ribs, stanchions, guys, cords, etc., including 5 square feet for the body of the operator, was 44.92 square feet, reduced, however, by reason of the rounding of the parts to an equivalent of 33.28 square feet, which area, multiplied by the pressure, would give the head resistance; that the apparatus would require a relative speed of 25 miles an hour (3.06 pounds per square foot pressure) in order to float it at an angle of incidence of +2 degrees, and

*Plate IX.*

Fig. I. — CHANUTE'S LAUNCHING WAYS.

Fig. 2. — See p. 58.

Fig. 3. — See p. 58.

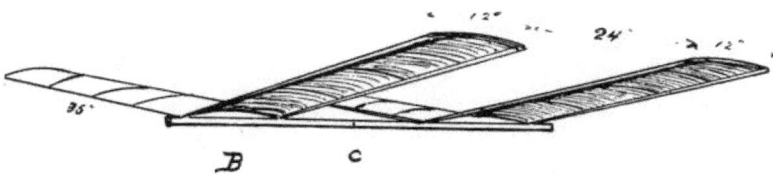

Fig. 4. — See p. 62.

Intentionally blank as was the original edition.

that, therefore, if Lilienthal's coefficients were used, the total resistances would be :

Head resistance, 33.28 sq. ft. $\times$ 3.06 lbs.             = 101.83 lbs.
Tangential component, 266 sq. ft. $\times$ 3.06 lbs. $\times$ 0.008 = 6.51   "
Retarding component, 320 lbs. $\times$ (sin 2° = 0.035) = 11.20   "

Total,        119.54   "

So that the angle of descent might be expected to be :

$$\frac{320 \text{ lbs.}}{120 \text{ lbs.}} = 1 \text{ in } 2.67 \text{ or } 22 \text{ degrees.}$$

These calculations were closely verified, as in the case of the other two machines.

It was the 15th of September (1896) before a proper wind served. It then set in from the north about noon and blew 28 miles an hour. The apparatus was accordingly placed in the ways, tested as to fit by running it up and down restrained by head and tail ropes, and then it was placed upon the level portion of the ways facing the wind. Additional guy lines were fastened to the wings, and Mr. Butusov got into the machine. The guy lines were manned, and the apparatus was suffered to rise 2½ to 3 feet above the ways, in order to test its balancing and the degree of control of the operator over its movements.

This appeared to be complete. A very slight step to the front or rear sufficed to depress or to raise the head of the machine, and the side motions were equally sensitive. The support was found to be ample from a 28-mile wind, and it was apparent that the great range of motion provided for the operator would give him command of the machine at all angles of incidence. The apparatus was then hauled down by the guy lines and settled back upon the ways squarely, resting thereon by means of four sliding shoes projecting from the machine on a line with the top of the boat-like body. It is shown in that position by Fig. 1, Plate IX.

It was desired next to launch it in ballast, and also to test it as a kite, and preparations were begun for that purpose ; but a small rip having been discovered in one of the wing coverings, and a buckling in one of the braces, it was thought more prudent to repair these before proceeding further, and the machine was removed from the ways.

The wind changed to the south-west in the night, but on the 17th it again blew from the north, with a speed, however, of but 12 miles per hour. In the hope of its freshening, the machine was got into the ways, loaded with 130 pounds of sand in bags, and rigged as a kite, by fastening a bridle to the keel of the boat and leading therefrom a long rope passing through a pulley fastened to a post in the sand, 250 feet away on the beach. This rope was handled by four men, with instructions to run with it so as to take up the slack as soon as the apparatus left the ways. Four guy lines, hanging down from the front and rear, and from each wing of the machine, were likewise manned, in order to control the movements of the kite in case of need.

All being ready, the restraining line was cut and the machine slid down the tallowed ways and took the air fair and level. It went horizontally some 20 feet, but its motion was then checked by the friction on the sand of the kite line, which the crew, gazing open-mouthed at the sight, failed to haul in as the machine flew forward. This check was sufficient to overcome the initial velocity proper to the machine, and the wind (12 miles an hour) was insufficient to sustain it. The apparatus glided downward and landed squarely on its keel about 100 feet from the end of the ways, a descent of about 1 in 2. The tip of one wing struck the hillside, but no harm was done as it flexed. Some three or four of the stanchions of the boat frame were, however, broken. These were replaced in two hours, but the wind had fallen so light by that time that the experiment could not be repeated.

To test the apparatus properly a north wind of about 25 miles per hour was required. This did not set in again till just before the advancing season compelled the breaking up of camp and returning to the city. On the 19th of September the equinoctial storm set in and blew from the north-west 56 to 60 miles an hour. Another gale of 60 miles an hour blew on the 22d, ac-

*Plate X.*

CAMP CHANUTE, 1896, SOUTHERN SHORE OF LAKE MICHIGAN.

BLUE HILL OBSERVATORY, MILTON, MASS.
Founded by A. Lawrence Rotch, Esq.
See pp. 149 to 153, 157, and 170 to 172.

Intentionally blank as was the original edition.

companied by heavy rains.   These were followed by southerly winds, so that it was the 26th before the machine could be tested again.   A wind then set in from the north-east, with a speed of 18 miles an hour, and although this was quartering, instead of dead ahead as was desired, it was determined to launch the apparatus.   This was first attempted with the operator in the machine, but as the quartering wind greatly increased the friction of the launching ways and diminished the required initial speed, the operator was replaced by 90 pounds of sand in bags, and a rope was fastened to the front of the machine in order to increase its velocity by pulling thereon.   The apparatus went off, but as soon as it had fairly left the end of the ways, the quartering wind swerved the head of the machine around, and it took a descending north-westerly course, describing a curved path. The tip of the left wing then struck the top of a tree, swinging the machine around further, and then this same wing struck the hillside and was broken.   The machine then fell to the ground, landing upon its keel about 75 feet from the end of the ways, and a number of ribs and stanchions were broken, so that the repairs, if made, would probably have occupied a day or two.

It was evident that the machine was moderately stable; that on neither this nor on the previous trial would the operator have been hurt if he had been in the machine; but it was also evident that the apparatus, as then proportioned, glided at too steep an angle to perform soaring flight; that it would lose so much altitude when going with the wind that the loss would not be recuperated when turned to face the wind.   It was recognized that this, as well as the other two machines, could be modified so as to materially reduce the head resistance and thereby flatten the angle of descent, but the season was so far advanced, the weather so inclement, that it was decided to break up camp and to return to the city.   This was done on the 27th of September.

Such were the experiments.   They occupied an aggregate of seven or eight weeks in the field, they were carried on without the slightest accident to the operators, and they made manifest several important conclusions. The first is that it is reasonably safe to experiment with full-sized machines, if the methods and writings of Lilienthal be previously studied. The second is that experiments with full-sized machines, carrying a man, are likely to be more instructive and fruitful of eventual progress than experiments with models. The third is the inference that it is probably possible to evolve an apparatus with automatic stability in the wind, but that in order to do so, there must be some moving parts, apart from the man, in order to restore the balance as often as it is compromised. The fourth conclusion is that the problem of automatic stability will be most easily worked out with a light apparatus, so light as to enable the operator to carry it with ease, and so arranged as to enable him to use his legs in landing. The fifth conclusion is that it will require a good deal of experimenting to adjust the working parts, to regulate the springs, and to discover hidden defects, before it will be quite safe to try to perform soaring feats in the wind. The sixth is that the incessant fluctuations of the wind, which so very greatly complicate the problem of maintaining automatic stability, probably result from the rotary action of its billows, and future experimenters are urgently advised to study this action and to endeavor to meet it.

A word or two of caution may also be given. It is best to begin experimenting with a new machine in short and low gliding flights over bare and soft sand hills, but more ambitious flights and soaring feats should be attempted first over a sheet of water to mitigate the fall should anything go wrong. Experiments should not be tried in high or gusty winds, and the apparatus should be frequently examined and kept in constantly perfect order. Wire stays should be employed as sparingly as possible. Not only do they vibrate when the machine is under way, and so increase the resistance, but they get loose and allow the apparatus to become distorted. It is well to fly a model of a projected apparatus as a kite, but it does not follow that a satisfactory kite will make a good flying-machine, because the required angles of incidence are so different. A good kite will fly steadily at an angle of 20 or 30 degrees with the wind, but a good flying-machine needs to fly at an angle of 2 to 5 degrees to reduce the drift to the lowest possible.

I do not know how much further I shall carry on these experiments. They were made wholly at my own expense, in the hope of gaining scientific knowledge and without the expectation of pecuniary profit. I believe the latter to be still afar off, for it seems unlikely that a commercial machine will be perfected very soon. It will, in my judgment, be worked out by a process of evolution: one experimenter finding his way a certain distance into the labyrinth, the next penetrating further, and so on, until the very centre is reached and success is won. In the hope, therefore, of making the way easier to others, I have set down the relation of these experiments, perhaps at tedious length, so that other searchers may carry the work of exploration further.

One of Mr. Chanute's Gliders:
see p. 36.

# RECENT ADVANCES TOWARD A SOLUTION OF THE PROBLEM OF THE CENTURY.

By A. M. Herring.

Perhaps no subject offers more scope to the imagination than the benefits and changes for mankind which would result from a practical solution of the problem of manflight. At the same time there is probably no problem which the inventive skill of man has ever attacked which apparently offers, at first sight, more numerous and easy ways of unravelment, and yet which, on careful investigation, develops greater or more unexpected difficulties. In the beginning of experiment the methods apparently open might be roughly divided into four classes.

The first of these would comprise all those machines in which the whole or part of the weight was lifted by a balloon or gasbag; the second, all those forms of apparatus which were intended to sustain or lift their weight with screw propellers revolving on vertical axes; the third, those machines which were intended to sustain their weight (and that of the operator) on flapping or beating wings; the fourth, and last, class would contain the aeroplane, or more properly the *aerocurve* machines; for the aeroplane may now safely be said to have disappeared from competition with the more efficient form of surface.

The limitations of the navigable balloon are now pretty well recognized. To obtain a speed of even 20 miles per hour, a spindle-shaped envelope of very large size is necessary, and the result at its best is an exceedingly frail and bulky machine, whose ultimate speed capacity is insufficient for wind velocities which frequently occur even near the ground. Its chief defects are great bulk and extreme frailty; for the envelope, in proportion to its relative size, is not many times stronger than a

(54)

soap bubble. An instance may be cited in support of this in the large navigable balloon built for the Antwerp exposition, which became tilted up during a trial, when the rush of gas to the higher end burst the balloon.

The future utility of the navigable balloon is still the subject of differences of opinion; it is, however, certain that whatever may be its ultimate practical advantages as a flying machine, the drawbacks of enormous size and frailty are sure to offer a considerable offset to them.

The vertical screw machines have much to recommend them, but there are far greater difficulties offered to their production than would be supposed. The ability to rise directly into the air from any given spot would be an exceedingly desirable quality. And hence we find that the great majority of experimenters who attack the problem of dynamic flight begin here, starting with a plan of some modification of this type of machine. The stumbling-blocks, however, are soon met. Not least among them is the fact that when the surfaces which form the blades of the screws are revolved over one spot (as they must be to rise directly into the air) they do not give any considerable lifting effect in proportion to the power consumed; for where one might from the theory even of the aeroplane expect a lift of possibly 100 pounds per horse-power, the best result the inventor can produce on a practical scale is pretty sure to be less than one-seventh of that figure. In fact, the lift with the lightest engines we can build is likely to be but little, if any, more than the weight of the machine itself. With engines weighing much more than 4 or 5 pounds per horse-power (250 times as powerful weight for weight as a man), practical success with this type of apparatus is not possible.

The third class, or the beating wing machines, are subject to the same disadvantages in regard to the enormous power required as those of the vertical screw type. In addition to this, the question of maintaining a stable equilibrium in windy weather still further greatly complicates them, so much so, in fact, that there is but small hope of practical machines operated on this principle ever being produced.

It is unnecessary to point out that any combination in a machine of the principles involved in either of the above three classes would still subject it to the fundamental objections of at least one of the classes.   These objections are so formidable that to the great majority of the foremost workers in this field, there now appears but one main principle left, and upon this there is an ever-increasing hope, if not certainty, that flight will be accomplished.   This principle is the one which underlies the aeroplane and aerocurve; namely, that when a thin surface is driven rapidly through the air, and is slightly inclined to its path, the equivalent of a pressure is developed on the side which is exposed to the air current — *i.e.*, the under side — which is much greater than the driving force necessary to produce it.   If an arched surface (arched in the line of motion) with the hollow side undermost be substituted for a plane, we have an aerocurve.   Its chief advantage is that it possesses a higher efficiency.   Another but minor difference is that it is not necessary to incline an aerocurve in order to develop a pressure on the hollow side when it is moved through the air.   [What is spoken of here as a pressure on the under side is chiefly a partial vacuum over the upper surface.]

The one advantage which the dynamic or power machine of the aerocurve type has over the vertical screw is the fact that it can, through the agency of the surfaces, convert the relatively small push of the screw propellers into a much larger lifting effect.

It is interesting to note that the first approach to human flight of modern times was attained only by the use of the aerocurve, when early in 1894 the late Otto Lilienthal, of Berlin, Germany, built a huge bat-like machine, with curved rigid wings, on which he was able to "slide" downhill on the air, 150 feet or so at a time.

Practice with this machine soon enabled him to start from very high places, and his flights became correspondingly longer.   Early in the beginning of these trials, he became aware, as his writings show, of the enormous power and disturbing effect which those ever-present irregularities in the wind produce, and which, in a large measure, were the cause of his losing his life—a sad accident which has taken from the field of aerodynamics one of, if not, *the* ablest of its workers; for both the practical and theoretical work of Lilienthal in the new science is of the greatest value, and will be so recognized when more generally understood.

In his first articles Lilienthal repeatedly cautioned others against attempting to glide in winds which exceeded 7 metres a second (about 15½ miles an hour), as being excessively dangerous. However, when he made the improvement on his machine of superimposing two smaller surfaces and thereby reduced the " tip to tip " measurement from about 24 feet to 18 feet, the diminished leverage upon which the gusts could act enabled him to sail in stronger winds, so that he even experimented in winds of 22 miles an hour. This, without further improvement in the automatic stability of his machine, was an unwise thing to do, and the accident which occasioned his death, on the 9th of last August, is, more or less correctly, attributed to it; nevertheless, the immediate cause was undoubtedly the result of defects in the machine itself, which had been allowed to deteriorate and get out of repair. In his double-deck machine the upper surface was joined to the lower one by two or three small vertical posts and numerous wires. Probably some of these wires had become rusted or so weakened that they broke when the machine was struck by a heavy puff, and so allowed the upper surface to tilt back and suddenly stop the headway of the machine, but not that of the unfortunate operator, who swung round and round over the apparatus as it pitched to the ground. This tendency to revolve over backward is frequently set up by a very strong sudden gust striking the machine squarely in front; it can, however, be counteracted by a quick movement of the operator's body and legs toward the front. A serious defect in the design of the Lilienthal apparatus is here seen, for on it the operator's position is somewhat strained, and his movement very limited, owing to the fact that he is obliged to hold to a small bar with both hands, while his weight is carried on his elbows, which rest, a little farther back, on a portion of the main frame. (See Plate IX., Fig. 2.)

These defects suggested themselves to the writer when, in the summer of 1894, he built a machine similar in many respects to that of Lilienthal. It differed from his in two important particulars: first, the upward movement of the horizontal tail was limited; second, the range through which the operator could shift his weight was nearly three feet instead of about eight inches. To obtain this range of movement the weight of the body, when in flight, rested upon two horizontal bars fitting under the arm-pits. (See Plate IX., Fig. 3.)

No very startling results, however, were obtained with this machine or with the three subsequent ones, the longest flight attained being only 187 feet in length; experiment with these machines, nevertheless, furnished a great deal of valuable information. No one who has not experimented with a machine of the Lilienthal type can form any accurate conception of the tremendous power and lifting effect which 130 to 150 square feet of concave surface can exert. It is with an apparatus of this kind that a novice first becomes fully aware that no wind is anything like constant, and that the power of those much-talked-of " gusts " is real, and not imaginary.

Any one wishing to begin experiment with a gliding machine cannot be too cautious in the selection of an experimental station. Nothing could be more dangerous than to start from a flat roof or a precipitous cliff, or to begin experiment in a locality where surrounding objects, such as hills, buildings, or even large neighboring trees, are likely to break up the wind into swirls and eddies. What is most desirable — in the beginning, at least — is a hill surrounded by country that is as level as possible. Both the starting and landing points should be on comparatively soft earth, free from stones, bushes, and snags. Perhaps the best station of all is to be had where there are high, bare sand-hills or dunes, facing a large body of water. The slope of such a hill (to a beginner) is of as much importance as anything else; it must be steep at the top and run off gradually as it nears the bottom so that when he has gained proficiency enough he may start from near the top in calm weather and yet have his flights always close to the hill-side. If this be so and the soil be comparatively soft, the operator can easily save himself from a dangerous fall which might result from a poor start or a breakage of the machine.

In first experiment with a full-sized gliding machine, a man's natural instincts irresistibly impel him to move in the wrong direction when the balance of the apparatus is disturbed. It is, therefore, at first, impossible to distinguish between effects produced by one's own errors and those produced by wind changes, but in time three separate causes of unsteady flying become easily distinguishable from each other; namely, improper adjustment of the machine, errors of the operator, and changes in the trend, velocity, or direction of the wind.

When the mastery of the machine becomes about as perfect as possible very much of this unsteadiness disappears; nevertheless, with a wind as steady as winds ever are, — even after having blown for hundreds of miles over absolutely level prairie, or, as in the case of our later experiments, having come in an unobstructed path for several hundred miles over the waters of Lake Michigan, — we found that the effect was by no means a steady one, but was such as to indicate that they were broken up into an inconceivable number of irregularities in pressure, velocity, and direction, in spite of the fact that a light anemometer showed fluctuations in velocity of seldom more than 10 or 12 per cent. in readings of 5 seconds' duration, taken 10 to 20 seconds apart.

In a wind of 9 to 10 miles per hour with a simple machine of the Lilienthal type the disturbances of the wind are barely noticeable, but at 12 miles they are quite apparent, at 14 miles they require considerable practice to combat, at 16½ miles, even with best skill at command, a flight is more or less risky; and when the wind blows above 18 miles per hour it is dangerous, even with a total load of 182 pounds (machine, 27 pounds, operator, 155 pounds) on 130 square feet of surface.

Nothing, perhaps, is more surprising than the power which a gust in even a 14 or 15 mile wind will occasionally exhibit, such, for instance, as sometimes happens to an inexperienced or careless operator, who, in facing the wind with the machine preparatory to making a start, suddenly finds himself lifted anywhere from 2 to 10 feet above his starting place.   These flights are invariably backward, and are due to mismanagement in allowing the wind to catch under the surface of the machine while the operator is too far back on it to exert a proper control.   In the hands of a skilled person, the flights, in mild winds, generally appear to an on-looker as remarkably smooth, and even in spite of the fact that the operator is seen to frequently shift his position on the machine with considerable rapidity; yet in slightly stronger winds — those of 15 to 16½ miles per hour (mean velocity) — the irregularities become very perceptible to the spectator, who may sometimes see the apparatus rock and toss not unlike a ship in a rough sea.

To appreciate the causes which render a gliding machine, or in fact any machine of the aerocurve type, unstable, it is necessary to understand, in a measure, both the peculiarities of the wind and the effect they have on the position of the centre of pressure of the surfaces.

In order for any apparatus in free air to be in equilibrium it is necessary, of course, that the centre of pressure should be in the same vertical line as the centre of gravity.   It is not, as many believe, absolutely necessary that the centre of weight should be beneath the sustaining surfaces; this may be demonstrated by trying the small paper model shown in Plate XII., Fig. 1, which, if not weighted too heavily, will always fly with the " fin " side up, even if dropped with the weight and fin side undermost.

When a surface is inclined to the air through which it is moving, the lifting pressure is not uniform, but is very much greater toward that edge which is first struck by the current. On a square *plane* 100 inches on a side, the centre of all the lifting pressures may be anywhere between the centre of figure and as far forward (apparently) as 14 inches from the front edge, according to the angle and speed at which the surface is presented to the air.   The travel sidewise might be even more, granting that gusts may come from either side. With an aerocurve the travel is probably seldom more than $\frac{1}{5}$ as much as it would be with a plane. In practice with any ordinary gliding machine of large surface it is found that the gusts come from any quarter: in front of the apparatus, from the extreme left to the extreme right, and in a wind of over 22 miles per hour they follow each other with such suddenness and with such extreme changes that it is absolutely impossible to shift one's weight in time to counteract them. These conditions, which had to be met, made it imperative to seek for automatic stability along very different lines from any that had heretofore been tried.

The changes or gusts which have the most influence in disturbing the machine are seldom of more than half a second duration, and oftentimes they last less than half that time; yet in so short an interval, it has frequently happened to me, in my experiments with my first three gliding machines, that in less than half a second the lateral equilibrium was so far disturbed that the lateral axis of the machine would make an angle of 35 to 40 degrees with the horizontal. At other times, the angle of advance (the angle at which the surfaces are presented to the air) was so much increased that nearly every bit of the headway was destroyed. On two occasions, the change in direction, both vertically and to the side, was so violent and sudden as to shake my hold loose of the machine.

During my last flight on a Lilienthal type of machine, while experimenting in a wind of about 18 miles an hour, the machine was struck twice in quick succession by a gust from the right. The first impulse raised that side until the apparatus stood at an angle of about 40 degrees; the second impulse, which came between $\frac{1}{4}$ and $\frac{3}{4}$ of a second later, increased the inclination to nearly a vertical one, so that one wing pointed to the ground and the other to the zenith. Anticipating a complete overturning of the machine (as did happen) I let go my hold and dropped to the sand below, a distance of not more than 12 or 14 feet, where I landed on my feet, but on the left wing of the overturned machine, which had drifted under me as

I fell. This accident damaged the machine so much that it was not rebuilt. We recognized from these experiments that the disturbances increased much more rapidly than the mean velocity of the wind; also that in winds of 18 miles or over, it was impossible for a man to shift his weight far enough and rapidly enough on a single surface machine to keep it in proper equilibrium under all circumstances.

In addition, the conclusions were reached, first, that the angle of advance *must* be automatically maintained, with almost absolute certainty, at a very small angle; second, that the lateral equilibrium should also be largely, if not wholly, automatic, and be maintained by some more effective method than a dihedral angle between the surfaces, or by placing the operator far beneath the apparatus. The first of these is considerably the most important, as disturbances of the angle of advance generally entail disturbances of the lateral equilibrium as well.

In the beginning of experiment to obtain longitudinal stability, three clearly defined methods (each with its own limitations developed by experiment) appeared open.

The first and simplest method is to find such a surface, or grouping of surfaces that the displacement of the centre of pressure is very great for very small changes of the angle of incidence; the second method is to find such a form of surface that its centre of pressure remains in one spot, no matter from what angle the relative wind may come; the third method is to provide a separate mechanism to either take up or counteract the disturbing effects of the wind changes.

The first method may be said to have been practically attained (as far as it is attainable by such an arrangement) in the various modifications of the Hargrave kite, and also in its predecessor, the Brown biplane, or, a little better still, in what might be called a " bicurve,"— that is, a biplane machine on which slightly arched surfaces have been substituted for planes. Such a model is shown in Plate IX., Fig. 4, B being the front aerocurve. This model will maintain a very good equilibrium for gliding flight so long as the centre of gravity is anywhere between C and the rear edge of B; but each change in the position of the centre of gravity corresponds, of course, to a different angle of flight, *i.e.*, to an angle at which the centre of pressure of the combined surfaces coincides with the vertical line through the centre of gravity of the whole apparatus.

The centre of pressure travels toward B as the angle of flight is diminished, and in the reverse direction when it is increased. This great range in the possible position of the centre of pressure is a measure of the corresponding change in efficiency which the rear surface undergoes at various angles of flight. This efficiency diminishes very rapidly as the angle of flight is diminished; at very flat angles its useful effect disappears altogether. Not only this, but at small angles of incidence, those under 8 degrees, the longitudinal stability of the arrangement disappears as well. From many experiments with gliding models of this type I found it impossible to obtain glides which represented a travel of over 4 lineal feet for each foot of height lost, unless the model was so weighted that no part of the weight rested on the rear surface. Also, that the power required to support any given weight at an angle of 15 degrees or less is about *twice* as much as would be needed on superimposed surfaces of the same size held at the same angles of inclination.

When the model shown in Plate IX., Fig. 4 (or any similar one) is so loaded that each surface must carry about half the total weight, the apparatus will take up an angle of about 26 degrees with the relative wind. Under this condition a dynamic model would require between 40 and 46 per cent. of its weight in thrust to keep it "afloat," or if liberated as a gliding model it will travel forward a little over twice as far as it descends vertically. At the flattest angle, about 15 degrees, at which it maintains a good equilibrium, it will glide only 3 to 3¼ times as far as it falls.

As the rear surfaces in an apparatus with following surfaces come more and more in the "wake" of the front elements, the relative supporting effect of the rear becomes less and less as the angle of flight is diminished. Thus, through the phenomena of "interference," the relative efficiency (as a lifting factor) of the rear surfaces becomes greater or less (as the angle of flight is increased or diminished) — a corresponding travel of the centre of pressure results which maintains the longitudinal equilibrium, but at the expense of extra weight of apparatus and considerable additional power.

This fundamental principle — that of interference — underlies the stability of the Malay, Eddy, Bazin, Lamson, Chanute, and Hargrave kites. It is still further applied in the three last named, in which the vertical keels form pairs of Brown's "biplanes," which maintain the lateral equilibrium as well.

It would seem that one might be able to avail of the wonderful stability which a system of following surfaces exhibits, by so grouping the surfaces *vertically* as well as horizontally that they could not interfere. It is comparatively easy to so space them that interference is practically avoided, but from several hundred experiments in this direction I have invariably found *that the automatic equilibrium is always impaired in direct proportion as the front and rear surfaces cease to interfere.* The further conclusion arrived at from these experiments was that in following surface machines, a low efficiency is essential to insure safe equilibrium. Quantitively this efficiency is so low that probably less than 30 pounds can be carried per horse-power when the surfaces are loaded to a greater extent than one pound per square foot of area. Consequently, though dynamic models might be made that would work satisfactorily on this plan, a full-sized machine to carry even one man would offer no such encouragement to its projector, chiefly because the weight of a machine increases much more rapidly than its surface or supporting power. Following surfaces therefore are not available.

Just as experiment and careful measurement made this fact clear, a new prospective method of obtaining automatic equilibrium began to open up. A study of the peculiarities in the travel of the centre of pressure of variously arched surfaces indicated the possibility of evolving such a form that the centre of the lifting pressures would remain in the same spot for all angles of inclination. The result of much investigation in this line is shown in Plate XI., Fig. 1. Strictly speaking, this piece

*Plate XI.*

Fig. I. — See p. 65.

Fig. 2. — See p. 67.

Intentionally blank as was the original edition.

of apparatus is a gliding model, and as such in a wind of 30 miles an hour or less it possesses a perfect equilibrium, owing to the fact that the position of its centre of pressure is almost absolutely constant for all angles of incidence between plus 90 degrees and minus 20 degrees; the same is also approximately true whether the wind strikes from in front or "abeam." It will also fly as a tailless kite, but as such is somewhat inferior to the Hargrave, both in steadiness and in the "angle of the string," yet the lifting effect is probably four times as great per square foot of surface. The projected area of the dome [1] is not quite 6 square feet, yet in some experiments it has registered a pull of over 40 pounds on a spring-balance, and on one occasion repeatedly broke a cord tested to 69 pounds.

As a flying machine it would have the advantages of being able to sustain great weight on a very small surface, and would require but a slow speed to do so. A dome machine of only 9½ feet in diameter would be of sufficient size to carry a man in gliding flight at a speed (relative to the air) of only 20 to 21 miles per hour. But its drift is so great that it would not carry the operator horizontally more than 2¼ to 2¾ times the height from which it started. As a great thrust of the screw is far more costly in power than great speed, such a machine could hardly be a practical success. However, owing to the very low sailing-speed a dynamic machine to carry one man might be built which would fly; but it would be of little practical value, owing to the excessive power required, and its limited speed capacity. This line of experiment was therefore laid aside in the spring of 1896.

By way of explanation I may here add that from a great number of previous experiments with various devices — such as modifications of the drag rudder, gyrostat, and pendulum regulators — I had come to the belief (which all my more recent experiments have only served to strengthen) that *the action of any device to maintain a machine in safe equilibrium must be*

---

[1] The plan of the dome is nearly circular, being only about one-eighth longer across the wind than with it. The curvatures of the front to rear sections are (as near as possible) all similar, each having a rise of 24-100 of the chord length, and having its highest point 42-100 of the same distance from the front.

*such that it prepares the machine for each impending wind-change before that change actually occurs*, and that any device which tends to forcibly right the flying machine *after* it has departed from an even keel more often produces (in the open air) greater *unsteadiness* than the reverse. The reason for this is not far to seek. It lies chiefly in the fact that the most formidable, as well as the most frequent, disturbances met with in the natural wind are cycloid gusts or rotating masses of air which frequently give a machine (or model) powerful double impulses. These impulses are generally opposite in their effect, and succeed each other by irregular intervals varying from about one-fourth to one second apart; and, therefore, a regulator, such as a pendulum or gyrostat mechanism, which begins to act on the machine after it is disturbed, and continues to do so until it regains an even keel, is often the means of greatly augmenting the second impulse of the pair, or the first of a new gust which may strike the apparatus from a different quarter. I do not mean to say that such devices will not work at all; on the contrary, they can be made to give very good results in fairly mild weather, but they all fail in winds of much less velocity than those which any practical machine must be able to contend with.

This conclusion reached, it would appear that the methods left would be found only through a careful study of the wind-changes themselves. As before stated, I had become aware almost from the beginning of my gliding experiments of several distinct kinds of disturbances, the most formidable being very sharp, well-defined changes in the velocity and direction of the wind, which last but a fraction of a second and appear to come in pairs. Their distinguishing characteristic (besides their much greater suddenness and power) is, that in practically all cases they are preceded by a perceptible warning which generally consists of a slight strengthening of the wind followed by a momentary calm, which in turn is followed immediately by the "gust" in its fullest force. During the momentary freshening, the wind either comes from or veers in the direction from which the gust proper will strike. These changes can easily be

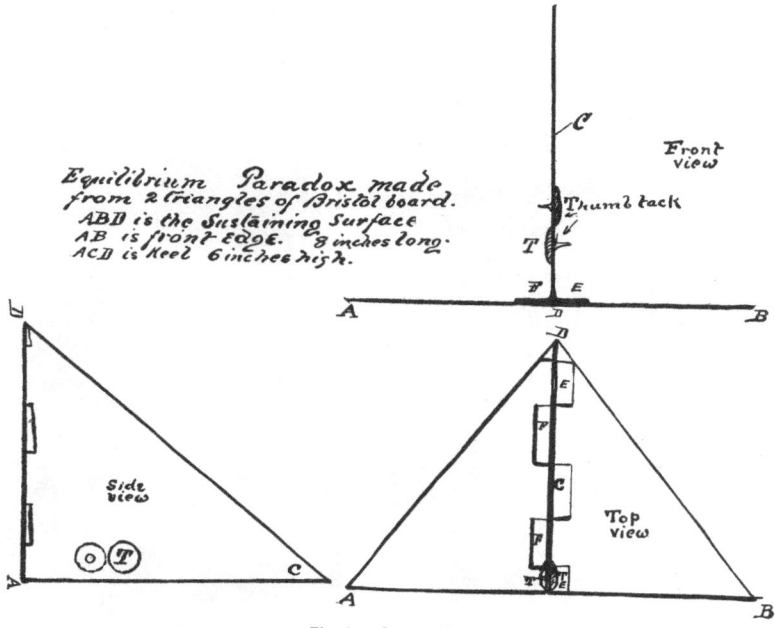

Plate XII.

Equilibrium Paradox made
from 2 triangles of Bristol board.
ABD is the Sustaining Surface
AB is front edge. 8 inches long.
ACD is Keel 6 inches high.

Front
view

Thumb tack

Side
view

Top
view

Fig. 1. — See p. 60.

Upright Struts
marked U
(should be larger)
1⅛ x ¾ for safety

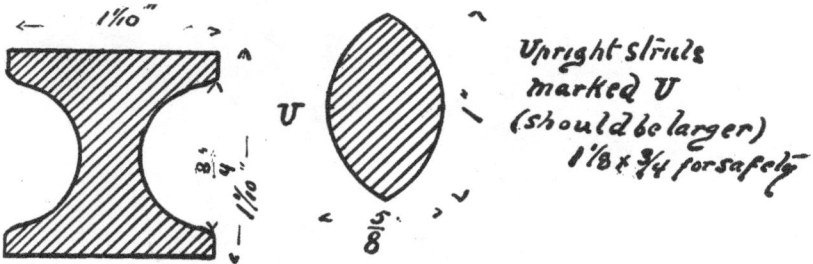

Tail Beam
max. section

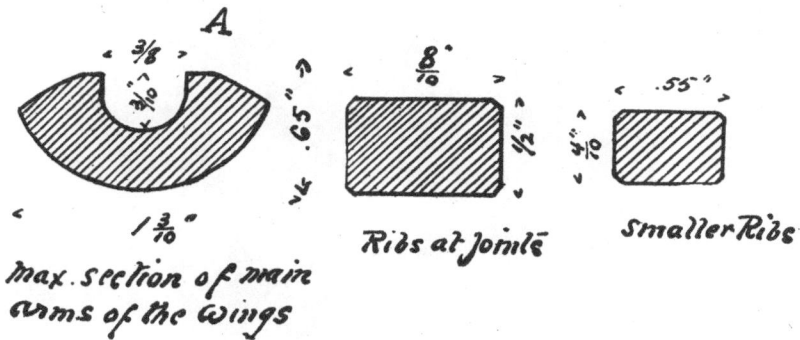

max. section of main
arms of the wings

Ribs at joints

Smaller Ribs

Fig. 2. — See p. 72.

Intentionally blank as was the original edition.

verified by an observer in a strong wind by noting the effects as he feels them on his face.

There are many observations which might be given to corroborate the theory that practically all the gusts which have any material effect in disturbing the angle of advance or the lateral equilibrium of an apparatus are of a rotary character; they are, in fact, nothing more or less than diminutive tornadoes; which travel, however, much more rarely on vertical axes than on diagonal or horizontal ones. In a few cases the axis of a gust is found to be horizontal and parallel with the wind. In the majority they are nearly horizontal, but across the direction of the mean wind. The direction of rotation is usually backward, *i.e.*, in the reverse direction that a wheel would have in rolling over the ground. In what may be called steady winds the swirls are of much greater diameter, and the out-flowing eddies, or the momentary freshening of the wind, precede them by a longer interval.

The observations which led to a recognition of the rotary character of the wind-changes also were the means which furnished an explanation of the action of certain simple devices previously found to work with success as far back as 1890 on a small dynamic model which has been illustrated in a previous issue of this Annual.[1] I was, therefore, not wholly in the dark in commencing experiments to produce a regulator which should prepare the apparatus to meet each particular " gust" before it arrived.

The horizontal regulator of the dynamic model was slightly modified to adapt it more closely to the new theory, and in May, 1896, applied to the kite shown in Plate XI., Fig. 2. This kite, which is here shown in a 28-mile wind, possessed such perfect power in maintaining the surfaces at a small angle with the wind, through changes which would otherwise prevent it from flying at all, that, in momentary freshening or changes, it would rise until the strings passed the zenith and made an angle of 6 to 8 degrees beyond the vertical. The average angle maintained by the surfaces with the horizontal varied between such narrow

---

[1] Aeronautical Annual, No. 2, pp. 94 and 95.

limits that it could not be easily detected by the eye. From a number of observations it was found possible to set the regulator to maintain an angle of between 2 and 3 degrees (above the horizontal), and calculations from the weight and surface of the kite, the pull on the string, and its angle above the horizontal show that the lift and drift of the kite correspond very closely indeed with the theoretical ones computed from the annexed tables.[1]

Later in the summer this regulating device was improved and its use extended so as to counteract the rotating columns whose axes were more or less vertical, and thus preserve the lateral equilibrium of the apparatus. With this change it was applied to the gliding machine shown in Plate XIII., Fig. 1. By its use the safe limit of wind in which experiments could be carried on was raised from 16½ miles per hour (with the simple Lilienthal, or 20 miles with the Lilienthal double deck) to over 30 miles, and with it the maximum length of flight was increased from 187 feet to 359 feet; at the same time the rocking and tossing of the apparatus was reduced to such an extent that an on-looker could not in any of the 150 to 200 flights detect that the apparatus in flight ever departed from an even keel, either laterally or longitudinally, — i.e., the angle of advance was maintained perfectly at the very flattest angle. It is evident from repeated measurements that this angle never exceeded 4 degrees with the relative wind.

The difference in the amount of ascending trend of the wind at different times and at various points in front of the hill made great differences in the length of flights. The results of an average flight in calm air are here given:

Net projected area of 2 supporting surfaces, 134 square feet; size, 16 feet 2 inches × 4 feet 4 inches.

Net area of horizontal tail (which receives a pressure on its upper side), 19 square feet.

Weight of machine, 23 pounds.

Weight of operator, 155 pounds.

---

[1] See page 178. [These tables were computed in English measures from data and fundamental formulæ given by the late Otto Lilienthal.]

Plate XIII.

Fig. 1. — See p. 68.

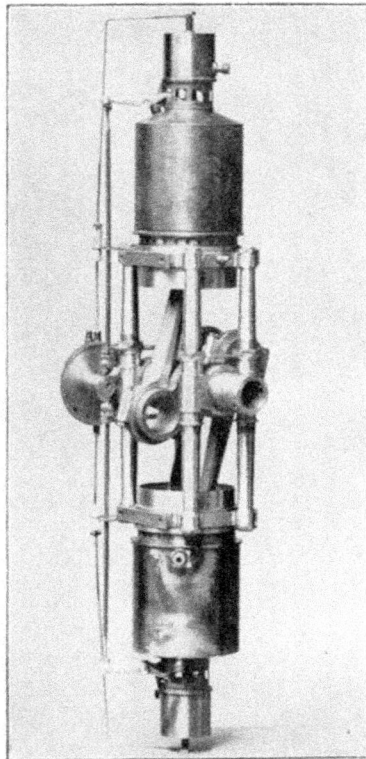

Fig. 2. — HERRING'S MOTOR. See p. 72.

Intentionally blank as was the original edition.

Pressure on upper side of tail (acting as weight), about 7 pounds.

Total weight carried by 134 square feet, 185 pounds.

Total weight carried per square foot area, 1.37 pounds.

At the time of the following experiment the air was nearly calm, the only trace of wind was from the north-east; the flight was made by running downhill toward the north. Length of flight, 242 feet from last foot-print to first at landing; time of flight, 7.4 seconds (in the air); difference in level between points was 42½ feet. Speed of machine was therefore practically 22 miles an hour. The wind pressure is $22 \times 22 \times .005 = 2.42$ pounds per square foot. The proportion of this as a sustaining factor was $\frac{1.37}{2.42}$, or 57 per cent. By referring to the tables (see p. 178) hereto appended it will appear (see second column, opposite positive angle of 3 degrees and 4 degrees) that this amount of lift (57 per cent. of the normal pressure) corresponds to a positive angle of the surfaces of between 3 and 4 degrees, and by referring to the third column we find that the drift of the surfaces is (.0525 for 3 degrees and .0582 for 4 degrees) about .056 times the total weight of machine and operator and negative pressure on the tail, or $.056 \times 185 = 10.36$ pounds, which is drift of the surfaces alone; to it we must add the head resistance offered by the framing of the machine and that offered by the operator's body. The framing consists of 64 lineal feet of timber which forms the main arms of the wings; this has a thickness of ⅝ of an inch across the wind, and therefore exposes a cross-section surface of about 3.3 square feet. The upright posts are 64 feet in collective length, being on an average $\frac{6}{10}$ of an inch in width (across the wind). Their area is therefore practically 3.2 square feet. But as they are sharpened more or less to lessen the resistance they offer to the wind, the total area offered by the woodwork, instead of being $3.3 + 3.2 = 6½$ square feet, is equivalent to only 2½ square feet. Besides this the framings of the tail and vertical rudder expose an equivalent of half a square foot of surface. The regulator and its cords, bands, etc., expose .52 of a square foot, and 160 lineal

feet of wire .05 of an inch in diameter expose the equivalent
of .5 square foot more, making the total equivalent area exposed equal to 4.02 square feet.  This at 22 miles an hour would
offer a resistance of 4.02 × 2.42 = 9.73 pounds; to this must
be added the resistance offered by the 5 square feet of the
operator's body, arms, and legs.  This brings the total resistance to: Resistance of surfaces, or drift, 10.36 pounds; head
resistance of machine, 9.73 pounds; and resistance offered by
operator, 12.1 pounds; total = 32.19 pounds.  This moved over
a distance of 242 feet would consume 242 × 32.19 = 7,790 foot-
pounds, which would be furnished by the weight of the
machine and operator (178 pounds), descending through a
vertical distance of 7,790 ÷ 178 = 43 feet 9 inches, against an
actual measured height of only 42½ feet.  The difference in
energy can easily be accounted for in either of three ways:
First, a slight overestimate of the resistance offered by the
operator's body; second, the presence of a slight ascending
current of air; or, lastly, that the speed gained in running down
the hill at the start was greater than 22 miles an hour.  (It is
possible to gain a speed of 26 miles if the weight is about half
supported on the machine.)  It may be interesting to point
out in passing that the energy (7,790 foot-pounds) absorbed in
keeping the machine and operator afloat during 7.4 seconds
represents barely 2-horse power, but less than one-third of
this is drift of the surfaces.  It is, however, now pretty well
known that it would take at least 3-horse power to produce
a thrust of 32 pounds, even with as large screws as could be
conveniently carried on a machine of this size.

The details of the regulating mechanism of neither this nor
the "three-deck" machine have been here given, as they are
now the subject of applications for patents; nevertheless, to any
one wishing to repeat the experiments I shall be pleased to
give all the information necessary.[1]

During October I constructed a new machine of the same
general design as the "double deck," but provided with three
superimposed surfaces instead of two.  In this a considerable

[1] The author's address is, A. M. Herring, 372 East Ontario street, Chicago, Ill., U.S.A.

change was made in the mechanism which governed the lateral equilibrium. Instead of depending upon the power in the small eddies which precede a rotating gust to operate the machine, their power was used only to work the valves of a mechanism operated by compressed air; in this way the regulation (which is accomplished through a reflex action) became much more powerful and prompt. The tests of the new gliding machine showed that a considerable advance had been made, in that the limit of wind velocity in which flights were safe was raised from 31½ miles an hour to over 48, and the maximum length of flight increased from 359 feet to 927 feet (best) and 893 feet (second best); at the same time it was found quite safe to turn the apparatus and fly at a considerable angle with the wind. It was by this means chiefly that the length of flight was increased, as the longer flights were made while " quartering " on the wind; that is, the apparatus after starting (the start must always be made dead against the wind) was kept pointing at an angle from 15 to 35 degrees with the wind, according to the strength of the latter, while the apparatus itself moved along a course nearly, but not quite, at right angles to the wind. This enabled me to keep close to the hill-side and take advantage of the rising current of air flowing over the slope. In a few of the flights it would have been possible to have landed on a higher point than the starting one, owing to irregularity of the wind which occasionally raised me, after having gone several hundred feet, to a level above my starting place; these rises were only momentary, and all the flights as a whole were on a descending grade. As the slope both to the right and left had several clumps of small trees which it was necessary to steer over or around (according to the height at which the machine happened to be while it passed near them), these " quartering " flights were not made to any great extent.

With a machine on which the angle of advance is automatically controlled with a fair degree of accuracy, the steering requires but little more effort than a bicycle, and at the same speed, *i.e.*, above 20 miles an hour, I have much doubt in my mind whether a bicycle (on a level road) could be turned on a much shorter radius than a flying machine. It is possible to land within less than 5 feet of any predetermined spot if it be selected well within the range of flight of the starting place.

In a few of the glides with the last machine I attempted to carry an additional weight, in the shape of a bag partially filled with sand. This bag was fastened between the middle and bottom surfaces, and beginning with about 12 pounds, the weight was gradually increased until 41 lbs. were carried without materially shortening the length of flight. The heavier weight considerably increased the difficulty in landing in light wind, owing to the greater speed relative to the ground. In high winds it was of very little hinderance either in starting or landing. The object in view in experimenting with the weight was to ascertain the power required on a dynamic machine and to test the manageability of the apparatus with a weight equivalent to the necessary engines and supplies. The result was so very encouraging that I have since then commenced constructing the engines. One of the pair is shown in Plate XIII., Fig. 2. It develops (alone) about two-thirds of the total thrust-power needed; its weight is only twelve pounds; its action is, however, a little irregular, and on that account is still the subject of experiment; it is a gasolene engine of the Otto cycle type.

Not least among the interesting results brought out by these gliding experiments is the fact, which becomes more and more evident from repeated experiment, that there is a very great difference in the supporting power of the air, whether one faces the natural wind or advances through still air; for while a natural wind of 18 to 19 miles per hour is sufficient (over level ground) to support the double-deck machine and operator, and will even momentarily raise them directly in the air for a foot or two, the same machine requires a minimum speed of 22 miles to support the same weight at the same angle in still air.

On Plate XIV. are given drawings of the three-deck machine; another drawing will be found on Plate XII., Fig. 2, giving exact sizes of struts, etc., in cross-section. If built to scale the

Plate XIV.

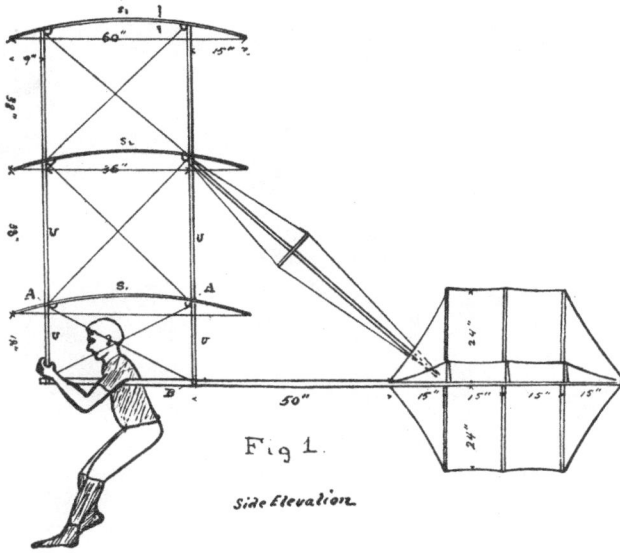

Fig 1.

Side Elevation

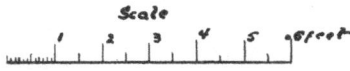

Scale

1    2    3    4    5    6 feet

- 15' 7½" -

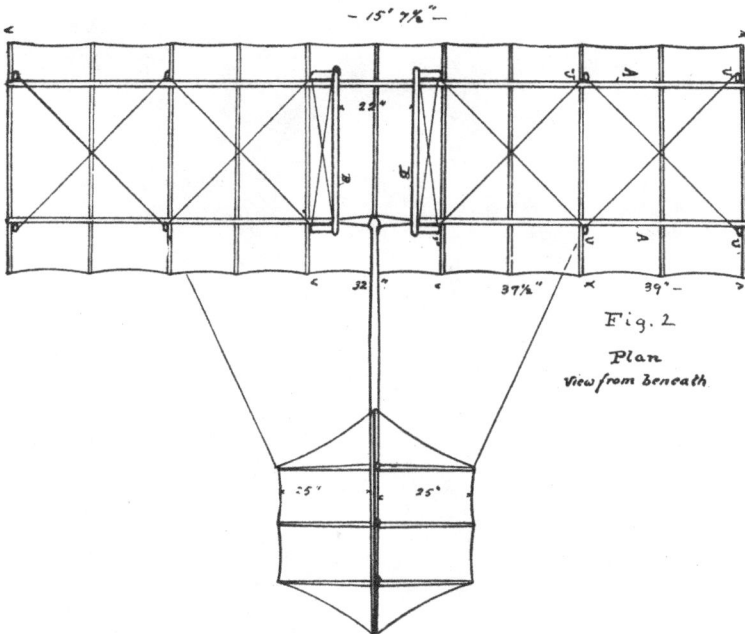

Fig. 2

Plan

View from beneath

WORKING DRAWINGS OF HERRING'S GLIDING MACHINE. See p. 72.

Intentionally blank as was the original edition.

machine will have 227 square feet (net) surface. This is, however, 40 per cent. more than a man of average weight ever
requires except in a calm or in winds of less than 10 miles an
hour. In winds over 12 miles an hour a beginner will get along
better with the upper surface removed. If this machine is built
on such a scale that the dimensions are only two-thirds of those
given, it will be of ample size (103 square feet surface) for
the average operator in any wind of over 25 miles an hour.
It is better not to reduce the size of main spars and struts at
all from the sizes given for the larger machine when constructing the surfaces on a smaller scale. The sizes given are for
the best grade of black or silk spruce *only;* this wood will stand
at least 16,000 pounds to the square inch; it must be straight
grain and entirely free from flaws.

There is, perhaps, no better sport imaginable than coasting
through the air, especially so where the flights are comparatively long. In moderate winds, of 18 to 25 miles per hour,
the path of the machine is often quite horizontal for a hundred feet or so after leaving the hill-side, until, in fact, the rising
current which flows over the hill has been cleared. If during
the first part of the flight an operator wishes to keep near the
ground he may do so by moving an inch or two forward on the
machine; he will find, however, that in thus sailing downward
through an ascending wind the speed increases at a tremendous
rate.

Perhaps the most trying ordeal is experienced when the
machine unexpectedly encounters a strongly ascending current of air which may raise the operator, in some instances,
40 or 50 feet above his line of flight. Such occurrences are
comparatively frequent in a wind of 30 miles or over, but are
not dangerous so long as the regulating mechanism remains
in working order, as the machine then retains an absolutely
level keel. I have twice been raised as much as 40 feet above
my *starting* point without either myself or those who were
on the ground being able to detect any change whatever in the
inclination of either axis of the machine. Considering the fact
that the rise through even such a distance seldom takes more

than 1¼ to 1½ seconds, the automatic stability of the machine would seem to be well attained.

After having adjusted the regulators, and repeatedly tested them in a number of short flights, and at the same time having found the correct position for his weight, all the beginner need do, after starting, is to keep as still as possible and he will make a very creditable flight. If it be necessary to steer to the right or left, moving the body over to that side and a little forward will accomplish the result. For ordinary steering it is seldom necessary to do more than stick out one leg toward the side to which you wish to turn. If you meet a very strongly ascending trend of wind it is manifested by an increase in the weight which appears to rest on your arms; in such a case the vertical rise may be greatly diminished by moving 2 or 3 inches forward of the normal position as long as the rise continues; it is better, though, to simply stick the legs out in front.

Descending currents of air diminish the weight on the arms and give one the sensation experienced in a quick-starting elevator on a down trip. So far, out of, possibly, over 300 trials with the regulated machines, a descending current has never brought the machine quite down but once, but even then the dropping speed was not too great to make a comparatively easy landing possible. On the other hand, the machines have been momentarily raised above their line of flight in probably 2 flights out of every 5. And in winds above 25 miles an hour the machines have risen above the starting point in as many as 75 per cent. of the flights. The highest rise was probably little short of 60 feet. The most difficult thing a beginner has to learn is how to land, *i.e.*, when to move back on the machine in order to check its headway; this knowledge can only be gained by actual experiment.

Plate XV.

GLIDING MACHINE IN FLIGHT.

Mr. Chanute's launching ways are seen in the distance.

Intentionally blank as was the original edition.

# OTTO LILIENTHAL.

A MEMORIAL ADDRESS DELIVERED BEFORE THE

*DEUTSCHEN VEREIN ZUR FÖRDERUNG DER LUFTSCHIFFAHRT,*
*NOVEMBER 26, 1896.*

BY KARL MÜLLENHOFF.

---

[Translated from *Zeitschrift für Luftschiffahrt.*]

THE irreparable loss which our Society has sustained in the death of Otto Lilienthal is still fresh in our memories. We all remember distinctly the untiring character of him who united the definiteness of aim which characterizes manhood with all the ardor and enthusiasm of youth.

For a long time, more than ten years in fact, Lilienthal was a member of our Society, and only a few of our oldest members can remember the whole of the energy which he devoted to our work. This is why I, who introduced Lilienthal into the Society, will endeavor to show what his membership really meant; all the more so, as it was I especially who was fortunate enough during the many years of mutual intercourse to really know the depths of this noble character and to learn to appreciate it. During this long period I had the good fortune to be initiated into all the phases of his studies of the problem of manflight.

Otto Lilienthal was born May 24th, 1848, at Anclam in Pomerania. Up to his sixteenth year he went to the Latin High School of his native city; in 1864 he entered the Potsdam Technical School; after graduation from this institution in 1866 he began the study of civil engineering by a one year's practical course in Schwartzkopf's machine shops. From 1867 to 1870 he was a student at the Berlin Technical Academy, and he had just been graduated from that academy when, in the summer of 1870, the beginning of the Franco-Prussian war called him into the service.

He served as volunteer in the Fusileer Infantry Regiment of the Guards, and was with that regiment at the siege of Paris. After the campaign was over he took a place as civil engineer in Weber's machine shops at Berlin, and was afterwards, from 1872 to 1880, engaged in the large machine shops of C. Hoppe, of Berlin.

In 1880 he started a machine factory of his own, and succeeded, in the course of time, in bringing it to a flourishing condition by his energy and inventive powers.

The products of his machine shops were of great variety. One of his inventions was the construction of light steam motors with serpentine pipes. He also made a specialty of marine signals. His achievements in these procured for him the silver State medal. The fog-horn which could be heard during the time of the Berlin trade exhibition near the Imperial ship was constructed and exhibited by him.

From his earliest youth he had been much interested in the subject of manflight, and as early as 1861, being only thirteen years of age, he began to make practical flying experiments, together with his younger brother Gustavus. The first wings made by the two brothers consisted of light flaps which were fastened to the arms; with these they attempted running downhill. The experiments were mostly made at night by moonlight, the young flying artists being naturally afraid of the teasing of their school-fellows.

The experiments which had been started in Anclam were continued in Potsdam. The two brothers constructed wings which were fastened to the back, and which moved up and down by throwing out the legs as in swimming. In 1867 and 1868 while in college, Lilienthal constructed a more complicated apparatus. In these experiments also his brother Gustavus took an active part.

The experiments interrupted in consequence of the campaign were taken up again as early as the autumn of 1871.

Lilienthal had seen that the negative results of previous flying experiments could be traced to the fact that it had been the custom to attempt the solution of the problem of birds'

*Plate XVI.*

OTTO LILIENTHAL.

Born 1848.    Died 1896.

"For thousands of years we human beings have racked our brains to unravel the mysteries of flight and we feel happy when we drink mere drops from the Fount of Knowledge, and here the storks seem to run riot in the art of flying, as if nothing in the world were easier."—See p. 89.

Intentionally blank as was the original edition.

flight trusting only to incomplete and even sometimes erroneous observations; or else to undertake the task of deriving the laws of the mechanics of flight purely theoretically without resorting to any observations at all.

Both methods would naturally lead to erroneous results. Lilienthal concluded to investigate the whole subject by means of exact experiment, examining scrupulously all the phenomena to be seen in the flight of birds. He began by measuring — by means of a long series of systematic measurements — the amount of the resistance of the air which the bird's wing has to overcome when in motion.

These experiments and measurements were for a long period made only by Otto Lilienthal, with the help of his brother. They showed the important and new result, that the curved wings, which nature, as we know, provides exclusively for her subjects, have a much more effective form than the flat surface hitherto so often constructed by men.

Besides this, Lilienthal was the first to point out the phenomenon which he thought was the probable explanation of the action of birds in sailing flight; that is, the existence of air-currents with upward tendency.

According to the observations made by Lilienthal these currents form on the average an angle of 3½ degrees with the line of the horizon.

Otto Lilienthal described the results of his numerous experiments in his pamphlet of the year 1889, entitled " The Flight of Birds as a Basis for the Art of Flying."

Shortly afterwards with the greatest zeal he again took up the practical attempts at flying which he had begun so long before. He had come to the conclusion that he could scarcely attain the solution of the problem of flight in his study, but that he must take the knowledge he had gained by observation and calculation out into the open air, to test with the wind, and in the element for which it was made, the apparatus constructed according to the theories he had developed. Theorizing alone would never bring about success. Brooding over and calculating about it would not bring one to the desired goal. One must draw up plans, build a machine, and then experiment with it. Lilienthal was right in pointing to the example of the bicycle to show how important practical experiments are in contrast to pure theory. Without doubt, our ancestors would have shaken their heads incredulously over the problem of the bicycle; it was first solved practically and now has come the theoretical solution. Of all the various methods of flying which nature shows us, sailing flight seemed the most worthy of imitation. It allows, as observation shows, the swiftest and most uninterrupted motion forward with a minimum of physical exertion. The solving of the mystery of this sailing-flight must therefore be the most important task of the flight technician.

The apparatus used by the experimenter in resuming his attempts in the spring of 1891 had the shape of birds' wings when spread out. The cross-section through the wing lying in the plane of the direction of flight was curved parabolically; the surfaces of the wings comprised in the beginning 10 square metres; they decreased gradually on account of various changes and repairs to 8 square metres. [The width comprised at its greatest 7 m. by 2 m.] The framework of the wings was formed of willow-wood; the covering was made of sheeting covered with wax. The weight of the apparatus was about 18 kilos.

In order to hold the apparatus the arms are placed in two cushioned openings in the frame, the hands at the same time grasping two corresponding handles. In this way the wings are perfectly under control, and may be safely leaned on in the air.

At first, of course, the flying experiments were made only from a low height and when there was no wind. Lilienthal made a spring-board on a large lawn in his garden in Lichtefelde which could be made higher by degrees; when first experimenting the board was but one metre high, later it was raised to two metres. On the spring-board he could take a run of eight metres in length. In spite of the jump the landing on the soft earth was gentle, so that a jump like this could be repeated many times without resulting in the least weariness or danger.

On having practised sufficiently the jumping off in this manner without wind, he selected another practising ground between Werder and Gross-Kreutz where several mounds of larger size, standing alone, made the experiments possible. Here it was found at once that in these experiments particular attention must be given to the wind then blowing. It is necessary when floating to move against the wind, for if one falls away from the wind, the pressure of the wind is felt, and the experimenter is not able to resist the one-sided effect. A vertical steering surface therefore had to be put on, thus enabling the apparatus to go against the wind.

On the grounds between Werder and Gross-Kreutz the jumping was done very frequently from greater heights and with winds of different force; a great deal of new experience was thus obtained. The final result was, that jumps of 20–25 metres' length could be made from the highest jumping point there, from a height of 5 to 6 metres. This was done when there was no wind as well as with winds of different force.

The difference showed itself particularly in the duration of the flight; the stronger the winds, the longer the journey in the air. The fact that landing when there is no wind is often a rather violent affair corresponds to what has been said, and it is therefore necessary to raise the wings a little in front shortly before landing, in order to mitigate the harshness of the shock and to prevent tilting over. This, however, refers only to flight when there is no wind; if the flight is against the wind, the landing on the ground is of an absolutely gentle nature.

The practising places not offering enough space to cover longer distances from greater heights, another spot, suitable for continuing the experiments, had to be chosen in the following year, 1892.

Such a place was found between Steglitz and Südende. The slopes here have a height of about 10 metres.

The experiments were made with an enlarged apparatus with a surface of 16 square metres and 24 kilos' weight, at a velocity of the wind up to 7 metres. He could take a start up to the jumping place, thereby obtaining a relative velocity of the air of 10 metres per second. Under these circumstances the first part of the sailing flight was almost horizontal; in its further course the line of flight sank considerably and declined rather suddenly at the end, as the wind loses a part of its force in the lower strata. In the most favorable case the length of the jump would be equal to 8 times the height of the jumping place above the landing point.

The surroundings of Berlin having a great dearth of good places for trying such flying experiments, Lilienthal constructed at Maihöhe near Steglitz a flying station of his own in the spring of 1893. A small declivity on this hill was arranged for a station for sailing flights. A tower-like shed was built, from the roof of which the flights were made, and which thus afforded a jumping place of 10 metres' height. The interior of the shed was used for storing the apparatus. The roof, which for the sake of a more secure start was covered with turf, sloped down, as did the declivity round the shed, towards south-west, west, and north-west. The apparatus showed a change as compared with that of previous years; it could be folded together, like the wings of the bat. It could, in consequence of this arrangement, be removed more easily and stored at almost any place.

It was only seldom, however, that the wind was favorable on the Maihöhe, and it was thus most important for the energetic continuing of the flying experiments that — in 1893 — Lilienthal succeeded in finding grounds which were suitable for his purposes in every respect. These are on the Rhinow mountains near Rathenow. Out of surrounding flat plough-lands there rises a chain of hills covered only with grass and heath, of up to 60 or even — as at the Gollenberg — up to 80 metres' height above the plain. The hills offer on every side descents, at an angle of from 10 to 20 degrees; and it is possible here to select a suitable position in whatever direction the winds make desirable, in order to glide above them through the air. The grounds really appear to be made for such flying experiments. The wind does not produce such gusts as at the flying tower at Steglitz, where one would always receive an irregular gust of wind from below, when passing the edge of the jumping

place.  Often enough this gust threatened to be fatal.  Besides,
this uniform acclivity permitted landing anywhere.

The wings which were used showed some changes as compared with those used previously.  Their weight is 20 kilos,
the complete weight just 100 kilos, the width from tip to tip
7 metres, the greatest breadth 2½ metres, the complete surface
14 square metres, a size which appears to be fully sufficient.

The wings are lowered when the experimenter runs downhill against the wind; at the proper moment he raises the supporting surfaces a little, so that they are about horizontal;
then while poising in the air he endeavors by suitably changing the point of gravity to give to the apparatus such a position that it shoots quickly forward while lowering itself as
little as possible.  After a short time a great progress in the safe
management of the apparatus could be observed.  Very often
sailing flights of 200 to 300 metre length were made from a
height of 30 metres; a great additional progress consisted in
the fact that he succeeded in directing the course of flight to
the right and left.  Changing of the point of gravity is effected
by stretching the legs in one or the other direction; even a
slight change of the centre of gravity brings about at once a
decline of the supporting surfaces towards the direction desired,
the pressure of the air also increasing on this side.  The direction of the course of flight then deviates to that side.  Several
times during the experiments the deviation from the straight
line of flight was carried so far that Lilienthal would at times
return to the starting place.

A place which was very well suited for his experiments, and
much more conveniently situated, was procured by Lilienthal in
the spring of 1894, in Gross-Lichterfelde near Berlin; he caused
a conic hill to be thrown up, which, having a height of 15
metres and at the basis a diameter of 70 metres, should admit
of flying experiments in whatever direction the wind blew.

On this place he tried with good success his new flying
apparatus, consisting of two surfaces arranged one above the
other.

He had come to the point already that the experiments regarding sailing flight could be considered as being completed,
and he proposed to take up the second task, viz., the imitating
of the rowing flight of birds.  A light machine, weighing in
all only 40 kilos and supplying 2½ horse-power for a short time
(4 minutes), was constructed and tested several times.  Lilienthal was therefore certainly justified in his words, when he de-
clared in a lecture given in July, '96, in the Berlin trade exhibition buildings, that he had strong hopes of being able to further
still more the development of the flying sport; but an accident
put an untimely end to his endeavors on the 9th of August.

He had made, on that fatal day, a very extensive sailing flight
on the Rhinow mountains, and thereby the special steering of
the movable horizontal tail had proved to be very satisfactory;
he then wanted to undertake a second flight of as long a duration as possible, and wanted to define the duration of the flight.

As a rule, such flights would last from 12 to 15 seconds.
He gave the timing-piece to his assistant.  According to the
statement of the latter, the flight was — up to half of the course
of flight — almost horizontal; then the apparatus had suddenly
tilted over in front, and had shot down rapidly from a height of
15 metres, being completely tilted over on the ground.  The
daring sportsman was dragged from the *débris*.  His spine being
broken, he died twenty-four hours later.  .  .  .

At present one cannot foresee what development may be in
store for the principles laid down by Lilienthal in the art of flying: one thing however is certain, that not one of the numerous
explorers and experimenters who have busied themselves with
the problem of flying has done so much as Lilienthal to bring
the difficult problem nearer its solution.  It has therefore been
justly emphasized, in the many accounts and debates which
Lilienthal's experiments have called forth over the whole world,
that he possessed three qualities in happiest union: He was
first a thorough mathematician and physicist, and had given important contributions to the theory of flight by reason of his
untiring observations and measurements of the resistance of
the air to curved surfaces.  Second, being a clever constructor,

and especially as mechanical engineer, he was able to build the apparatus himself as he thought best fitted for imitating the flight of birds.    Third, he possessed great daring and physical dexterity, so that he was in himself fitted for making experiments in flying.

Therefore his memory will be faithfully cherished by all those who have decided to labor on in the field of work which he made his own.

# OUR TEACHERS IN SAILING FLIGHT.

By Otto Lilienthal.

*Translated from Prometheus.*

---

I HAVE recently seen such wondrous feats performed in sailing flight that, as I now sit at my table to write, I do so with more enthusiasm than ever before; for the things which I have seen prove clearly and definitely that flight must be much easier than it is generally believed to be, if we only, with suitable wings, boldly trust ourselves to the wind. All perplexities concerning light motors, and speculations on the amount of power required for flying, are relegated to the background by the fact that the power of the wind alone is sufficient to effect any kind of independent flight.

If we had not those magnificent models in flying, those large and heavy birds which, without a flap of the wing, allow themselves to be borne by the wind, doubters would be justified, and we should lack the courage to attempt the solution of the problem with the perseverance which is necessary; but, as it is, the tangible results cannot be denied, there is a flight which does not require any effort, where only the shape and position of the wings must be right in order to float, circle, or sail in the air at any height or in any direction desired; therefore our confidence, notwithstanding many vain attempts, is always renewed.

But which are the birds best fitted as models in soaring flight? How can we best find a position for making fruitful observations?

If we go through the fields in summer, we see now and then a bird of prey circling about; then a swamp bird, of the larger kind, passing along arrests our attention: yet if one goes out on purpose for such observations, it may be that he will lie in wait for days in vain, or if a sailing bird comes in sight, it is very likely high up in the heavens and far away, so that little can be learned from it.

The Americans are proud of their buzzard which gives them such exhibitions in the art of soaring, but in order to observe this near at hand and to be able to study the effect of soaring, places of concealment must be arranged in the tops of trees and in rocks from which the observer may watch the motions of flight.

Things are easier for people living on the coast; the graceful soaring flight of the gulls can be frequently observed near at hand, as these birds are not very timid, from their being so seldom hunted.  But the best opportunity for studying soaring flight is to be had in the lowlands of Northern Germany, in the villages, where the stork lives his family life on the low roofs, unconcernedly showing off his art close above the heads of observers, and by his size giving the observer the clearest impressions of the shape and position of the wings.

But even at these stork nests it is tedious to wait for the moment when the old birds return with food for their young; it is generally only for a short moment, in the quick coming and going, that one can observe closely the flying or the soaring stork.

Observation is more productive when the young birds are fledging.  As soon, however, as they have learned to soar, which soon happens in windy weather, they do not remain in the vicinity of the nest, and one can look for them a long time in vain.

Being convinced that Father Longlegs is just made for our instructor in flying, I kept a great many young storks some years ago, whose attempts at flying have given me many explanations in flying technics.  As soon, however, as their proficiency extended to soaring, when rising above the tree-tops, they felt the magnificent bearing-effect of the wind, and ventured into higher regions, they joined other wild storks, and so ended all further observation.

While on a journey to procure these young storks a friendly man told me that there could be no better place for observing

these birds than the village of Vehlin, near Glöwen, on the
Berlin-Hamburg railroad, for there there were on every roof
two or three stork nests, and hundreds of storks circled above
them.

This address slumbered, probably, seven years in my note-
book, till last Easter I made use of the fine days to take a trip,
in company with my two boys, to Vehlin.   The road — a two
hours' walk — from the station of Glöwen led us through villages
in no way distinguished by a wealth of storks.   I began to
think the good man had played us a joke.   But on approaching the village of Vehlin, my two boys cried out, "Why, there
is a stork's nest!"    "There's another !"    "And another!"
"There are two on one roof !"    "Yonder are two more !"    Our
friendly adviser was quite right, for on the forty houses of this
little village were no less than fifty-four storks' nests, about some
of which the single pairs were yet fighting, while in some the
process of hatching had already commenced.

With the exception of an interesting combat between the
male storks which, rolled up like a ball, often rolled off the
roof, only separating in a fright on dropping into the yard,
there was not much to be seen that day.   Yet I was glad to
know of a place where in mid-summer, when the young storks
are fully grown, the most magnificent exercises in flying would
be observable.   I was not mistaken.   On going again to Vehlin
in August, almost the entire army of storks was to be seen in
the air over the village.   The day was sunny and windy, just
suitable for studying the soaring of these immense birds.

My observations result, so far, in ascertaining that in windy
weather, when the air in the lower strata has a velocity of about
six to eight metres, the stork does not move its wings at all,
and proceeds soaring or sailing in the air.

This soaring took place not only close above the roofs of the
houses, but also at so great a height that it was difficult to follow the birds' motion with the naked eye.   The birds flapped
their wings only when moving between the houses or trees —
that is, in places protected from the wind.   They soared in any
direction they pleased, against the wind, with the wind, or side-

wise. They circled in order to ascend quickly to higher air strata.

When instructing their young the storks fly mostly in smaller or larger companies, at different heights, flying over the village alternately with or against the wind. In some of the nests young birds were standing, which did not yet take part in the exercises. As soon as these latter saw their relatives fly away above them they would greet them in their own peculiar language, by laying their heads on their backs and rattling with their beaks. Generally some of those flying would descend from the rest to their young ones in the nest. If the flight in doing this had to be made from a great, windy height, it gave the impression that the stork found the descent more trying than the ascent.

To descend more rapidly the stork employs various manœuvres. The simplest is that of letting the legs hang, thus lessening the soaring effect by a resistance to the air. With a good sailing-wind, however, these means are insufficient, and head and neck have to be lowered, at the same time the wings are bent so low down as to form the perfect shape of a bell. This position, however, appears to cause the stork an effort, as it soon changes again to the outspread position. On attaining this, however, it again commences to ascend, and then it is seen, after a few vain efforts to come down quickly from the height, to employ a radical means for rapid descent. This consists of placing itself in a vertical plane; that is, with the point of one wing underneath, the point of the other above. In this manner it can, of course, shoot downwards like an arrow. In its downward rush, however, it changes several times from the right position to the left. Finally it takes once more the position of the bell, till it lands on the nests, where it is always received, after such feats of prowess, with a joyful rattle.

A good deal could be said about these drops, often from a height of several hundred metres, but we have less interest in the descent from the height than in the art of balancing in the air simply by means of outspread wings.

In order to observe this proficiency frequently close to, we

chose a point of observation on a farm which was blest with five
stork-nests, and from where we could oversee a dozen others.

The only means of lifting the last veil from the mystery of
soaring is to be able to frequently observe large birds at a near
distance in their soaring flight.

Three things are essential for soaring: a correct shape of
wing, the right position of wing, and a suitable wind. In order
to judge of these three factors and their changeable effect, we
have nothing but our practised eye to depend upon.

Just how much the cross-section of the wing is arched when
the stork is resting on the wind can be determined only by eye
measurement; similarly the position of the wing to the direction
of the wind and to the horizon. But when hundreds of storks
give one the opportunity to observe the same in clear weather
close at hand, what is seen is impressed so indelibly on the mind
that it enables one to draw correct conclusions as to the existing laws.

In general, one can say that when the stork flies with wings
spread horizontally and allows itself to be borne by the wind
alone, it is but seldom that a stronger gust of wind causes the
stork to draw in its wings.

The parabolic profile of the wings has a depth which I consider to be about $\frac{1}{20}$ of the breadth of the wing. The pinions
are mostly spread out, but do not lie in one plane; but the
more they are to the front, the higher are the points, certainly
because they would otherwise hinder one another in their
bearing capacity.

When in this position the stork passes slowly against the
wind above the observer, the head and neck are, as a rule,
stretched straight out; but if one imagines that soaring is possible in this position, that it causes little resistance, he will be
surprised to see a stork, sailing in this manner, suddenly, without changing its position, lay its head back and rattle joyously.
While we human beings are striving to find the proper shape
for the wings, building theory on theory, flying takes place
in nature in a wondrously simple way, quite as a matter of
course.

It is ever with a large surplus of flying capacity that nature has equipped her subjects. A stork which has lost some of its largest pinions does not for that reason sail less gracefully than its comrades.

Storks are not particular in the way they hold their pointed beaks and long necks, as has been observed already. One after the other sailed over our heads; one held itself to one side, the other kept to the other side, without any change in their flight. Here comes another one very slowly against the wind; just as it stands over our heads it bends its head to the left to take a minute survey of its wings, on which it puts its head quite to one side and begins in a most leisurely way to put the feathers on its left wing in order with its beak; meanwhile its graceful sailing-flight does not suffer the slightest interruption. We looked at one another surprised by this sight, as if we would say, " That is beyond everything ! For thousands of years we human beings have racked our brains to unravel the mysteries of flight, and we feel happy when we drink mere drops from the Fount of Knowledge, and here the storks seem to run riot in the art of flying, as if nothing in the world were easier." [1]

Afterwards I found out that a stork, putting beak, head, and neck back quite to the left, certainly changes the left wing a good deal more, but that, in this position, wherein head and neck are directly in front of the arm of the wing, to a certain extent a broadening of the left wing and therefore an increase in the bearing capacity of the same takes place.

One might therefore not be at all surprised if the balance in soaring be not disturbed. The young storks, which are known by their gray legs, betray themselves also in the air by their less sure flight; in soaring they are sometimes thrown here and there by the wind, and therefore take more frequently to flapping their wings than their red-legged parents, which understand in a masterly way how to meet every gust of wind.

---

[1] Wir Menschen quälen uns seit Jahrtausenden, hinter die Räthsel des Fluges zu kommen und sind schon froh, wenn wir tropfenweise aus dem Born der Erkenntniss schöpfen können, und hier wird von den Störchen in einer Weise mit dem Flugvermögen gewuchert, als gäbe es in aller Welt nichts Leichteres als das Fliegen.

Whoever observes minutely a stork, which is proficient in flying, sailing along at a moderate height, will notice a limited but almost uninterrupted turning and moving of the wings which apparently serve to exactly meet the pressure of the wind. Our eyes are riveted with admiration and wonder on each of these birds as they pass along. They skim and sail in the air, and their bodies, weighing four to five kilograms, appear to be borne by a magic power. Their whole behavior indicates that a flight like this is no labor, but rather akin to resting; their tameness lets them pass close to us; we can recognize each feather of their outspread wings. All deception as to the real cause of sailing flight appears excluded. That which is possible to these storks must also be possible to any other similarly formed flying body.

As the little swallow, which just now sails over the farm-yard through the broken window into the cow-shed, understands soaring on the same principles as the stork, so must, on the other hand, a larger apparatus, capable of bearing up a man, be able to sail on the wind, if it be of the right shape.

Of course such an apparatus alone cannot equip us for flying; the capability of using it, which is inborn with the stork, must be gained by us by laborious training, but even in this we can trust ourselves fully to our long-legged instructor. It shows us with what facility one can change the irregular blowing of the wind into bearing-power, provided we have the necessary practice. When the stork sails over the roofs of the houses one can see how it applies every gust in the air to its advantage. The higher it circles, the more tranquil and certain its flight becomes in proportion to the increasing uniformity of the wind.

A particularly fine spectacle is a stork remaining for a great length of time floating (remaining stationary) at one point in the air. This feat also, where all the forces are equally balanced, I saw performed by older storks only. These masters in the art of flying understand how to keep their position at one point even in high winds, as well as to shoot along with high velocity, all of which they perform by careful adjustment of their outspread wings.

The simplicity of the instruments with which nature obtains these wonderful effects in flying gives us hope that we shall come to a satisfactory solution of the problem.

Whoever needs incentive to labor with zeal ought to look up the little village of Vehlin in Ostprignitz in mid-summer, when the magnificent birds in their fine black and white garments sail majestically overhead, and are seen against the blue of heaven like emblems of liberty.

# AT RHINOW.

[The following is a translation of an extract from an article by Lilienthal in *Zeitschrift für Luftschiffahrt*, March, 1895.]

LILIENTHAL writes thus of the extreme care needed in making changes in an air-sailing machine:

My neglect of this circumstance I once came near paying dearly for. The winter before last I constructed several machines, the sustaining surfaces of which had an exact parabolic profile which almost coincided with the arc of a circle. The holding point for the hands and arms I placed in such a manner that the centre of gravity of the body was, on the average, situated one-tenth of the width of the wing in front of the centre of the surface. In my experiments made before Easter from the still higher mountains near Rhinow, I perceived that I had to bear with the upper part of my body a good deal towards the back to prevent my shooting forward in the air with the apparatus. During a gliding flight taken from a great height this was the cause of my coming into a position with my arms out-stretched, in which the centre of gravity lay too much to the back; at the same time I was unable — owing to fatigue — to draw the upper part of my body again towards the front. As I was then sailing at the height of about 65 feet with a velocity of about 35 miles per hour, the apparatus, overloaded in the rear, rose more and more, and finally shot, by means of its *vis viva*, vertically upwards. I gripped tight hold, seeing nothing but the blue sky and little white clouds above me, and so awaited the moment when the apparatus would capsize backwards, possibly ending my sailing attempts forever. Suddenly, however, the apparatus stopped in its ascent, and, going backward again in a downward direction, described a short circle and steered with the rear part again upwards, owing to the horizontal tail which had an upward slant; then the machine turned bottom upwards and rushed with me vertically towards the earth from a height of about 65 feet. With my senses quite clear, my arms and my head forward, still holding the apparatus firmly with my hands, I fell towards a greensward; a shock, a crash, and I lay with the apparatus on the ground.

A flesh wound at the left side of the head, caused by my striking the frame of the apparatus, and a spraining of the left hand, were the only bad effects of this accident. The apparatus was, strange to say, quite uninjured. I myself, as well as my sailing implements, had been saved by means of the elastic recoil-bar, which, as good luck would have it, I had attached for the first time at the front part of the apparatus. This recoil-bar, made of willow wood, was broken to splinters; it had penetrated a foot deep into the earth, so that it could only be removed with difficulty. I describe this accident so minutely because it is probably the worst which could happen in sailing flight; I wish to say that this is not the accident which gained publicity through the press, and which was the cause of a correspondence from all countries. The only outside spectators of this fall were the little girls and boys of the Stöllner schools, who had had vacation, and were looking on with their teachers at my experiments from the ridge of the mountain.

My brother, who also took part in these experiments and had been able to get a perfect side-view of my unsuccessful flight, said it had looked as if a piece of paper had been sailing about in the air at random. In my thousands of experiments this is the only fall of that kind, and this I could have avoided if I had been more careful.

If one uses the necessary precautions when making the experiments, any great danger is, strictly speaking, excluded. The use of a recoil-bar is, of course, always advisable.

In the very slight accident which a reporter who happened to be present brought into the papers in a greatly exaggerated and incorrect way, the elastic impact of the recoil-bar proved to be excellent. In this experiment a change in the curve of the surfaces came into account. I was occupied in testing wings of the strongest possible curves to make compara-

tive experiments regarding the influence of the amount of concavity on the bearing capacity.  I had already taken several
successful flights with an apparatus the concavity of which was
a little over $\frac{1}{12}$ of the breadth of the wing; then while sailing, the
apparatus was pressed down in front by a wind from above, in
the middle of the course of flight, by means of which it was run
to the ground.

With these strongly curved profiles the danger is, that the
surface being strongly inclined, the front receives some pressure
of the air from above in consequence of sudden changes in the
wind, and this would, of course, greatly diminish the stability of
the flight.  As has already been observed, it is not advisable to
extend the height of the profile beyond $\frac{1}{12}$ of the breadth of
the wings, in spite of the excellent sustaining qualities which
may so be obtained.

One can produce very safe working qualities with strong
power of sustentation with a height of profile between $\frac{1}{18}$ and
$\frac{1}{16}$ of the breadth of the wing.

As a matter of course, the more one penetrates into the
details of the technics of flight the more varied the points of
view will become.  This is the case even with simple sailing
flights which demand only a simple sustaining surface.  How
much more this will be the case in dynamic flight!  I have had
already enough impressions as to that.  But of this some other
time.

# THE BEST SHAPES FOR WINGS.

By Otto Lilienthal.

[Abridged translation from *Zeitschrift für Luftschiffahrt*, XIV. Jahrgang, Heft 10.]

THE results which we reach by practical flying experiments will depend most of all upon the shapes which we give to the wings used in experimenting.

Therefore there is probably no more important subject in the technics of flying than that which refers to wing formation.

The primitive idea that the desired effects could be produced by means of flat wings has now been abandoned, for we know that the curvature of birds' wings gives extraordinary advantages in flying.

The experiments on the resistance of air to curved surfaces have shown that even very slight curvatures of the wing-profile increase considerably the sustaining power, and thereby diminish the amount of power required in flight.

The wing of a bird is excellent not only because of the curvature of its cross-section, but the rest of its structure and formation also has influence upon the flight. Therefore the outline of the wing is certainly of importance.

It is probable that the form of the cross-section of the wing and flight-feathers (*Schwungfedern*) has a favorable influence upon the flight.

Experiments have not yet been made to show conclusively whether or not the feather structure of a wing endows it with a special quality whereby the sustaining power is increased. With investigators this has been a subject of conjecture. Therefore it is questionable (*auch fraglich*) whether we are wrong if, in constructing flying apparatus, we keep to the bat's wing, which is easier to construct.

Bats fly much better than is generally thought. Two early

(95)

bats, which I saw flying this summer in broad sunshine and in somewhat windy weather, sailed along so well without flapping their wings that I thought, at first, they were swallows. Of course on evenings when there is no wind, the bat must flutter continually. The early-flying bat is also called evening-sailer (*Abendsegler*) which indicates that its sailing flight has been marked.

The most important point as regards the form of the wing will always be the curvature of its profile. If we examine any bird's wing we find that the enclosed bones cause a decided thickening at the forward edge. The question now is, What part does this thickening play in the action of the curved surface? The thickening is quite considerable, particularly in birds which have long, narrow wings. An albatross in my possession has a breadth of wing 16 centimetres, the thickened part of which measures 2 centimetres; the thickness is therefore $\frac{1}{8}$ of the breadth of the wing. As the albatross is one of the best sailers, we can scarcely assume that the comparatively great thickness of the wing at its outer edge has a detrimental effect upon the bird's flight.

For a long time I have assumed that the thickening which all birds' wings have at the front edge produces a favorable effect in sailing flight.

.    .    .    .    .    .    .    .    .    .    .

By means of free-sailing models I have now learned that nature makes a virtue of necessity, that the thickened front edge is not only harmless, but in sailing flight is helpful (*sondern den Schwebe-effect nicht unerheblich erhöht*).

The experiments are easily tried. It is only necessary to make a number of models of equal size and weight, each one having a different curve in its sustaining surfaces. These models I make of strong drawing paper, the size of the surfaces being about 4 inches in width by 20 inches in length.[1]

The experimenter can let these models sail from any tower or roof in front of which there is an open space. Each model must be made to glide through the air many times until it

---

[1] **Drawings** of these models will be found on pp. 14 and 15, Aeronautical Annual, No. 2.

reaches the ground. Experiments must be made in the stillest possible air.

The lengths of flights are all noted down, and from a long series of experiments the arithmetical mean for each design is computed. The models having the best profiles will make the longest flights. In this way a reliable table can be made which will show the relative merits of the profiles, and will also show quite plainly in which direction the most useful form will have to be developed.

Until now I have endeavored to find out the best proportions for wings by constructing different kinds of sailing apparatus. In this way, of course, many important facts have been ascertained. The construction of full-sized apparatus requires a great deal of time and is expensive, therefore we must welcome a method which permits inquiry into the forms of wings in models which fly automatically. Besides that, it is not every one's business to throw himself into space in a sailing apparatus, although he who would succeed in practical flying can scarcely avoid this way.

Considering the fact that the most important thing is to ascertain what are the best qualities of the natural wing, — which is in every respect perfect, — these steadily sailing models offer every one an opportunity of engaging in experiments of this kind. Further, any one who takes up this kind of experiment will find great pleasure in watching the manœuvres of his small flyers, which often vie with the best sailers among birds. I can therefore recommend this occupation not only for the furthering of the science of mechanical flight, but also because it affords a most interesting pastime.

The few measurements made so far by this method are too incomplete to be fit, as yet, for publication. I am preparing, however, a systematic series of experiments, the results of which will be stated when the experiments are finished.

Meanwhile, I cherish the hope that this paper may be an incentive to others to make similar experiments, so that we may sooner reach the desired end.

NOTE. — This is a part of Lilienthal's unfinished work, which it is to be hoped will be taken up by many. The fact that he thought it well worth doing is significant. — ED.

# SAILING FLIGHT.

By O. Chanute.

[Begun in Aeronautical Annual No. 2.]

---

## PART II. — THE EXPLANATIONS.

MANY theories have heretofore been advanced to account for the paradox of sailing flight. The writer knows of some twenty-three different explanations, more or less complete; but most of them are fragmentary — rough casts, as it were, as to how the feat is accomplished, without qualitative or quantitative considerations. Indeed, all of them except Basté's and Vogt's lack the latter, and no one, so far as the writer knows, has published full mathematical computations showing just how the sailing bird is supported and propelled, at the actual measured speeds of wind and bird, and at the angles of incidence observed.

Before submitting some computations of my own, it seems desirable to first review the theories which have been advanced. These may be grouped under eight different heads, as follows:

1. Assimilates sailing flight to kite action.
2. Assumes rising trends in the winds.
3. Supposes different coefficients on front and rear of birds.
4. Surmises propulsion to be obtained by tacking and circling.
5. Believes energy to be derived from combination gravity and wind.
6. Believes energy to be drawn from the different speeds of wind strata.
7. Believes energy to be drawn from intermittency of wind force.
8. Believes energy to be drawn from variations in wind direction.

### 1. KITE ACTION.

*Count d'Esterno* in his book[1] and writings assimilated the sailing bird to a kite, in which the weight replaced the action of the string. He held that inasmuch as the area of the sus-

---

[1] " *Du Vol des Oiseaux.*" *Librairie Nouvelle.* 1864.

taining surfaces was greatly in excess of that of the edge surfaces (body and wings) which the wind acted upon, it was
possible for the bird to transform into forward propulsion
whatever surplus lifting effect he received from the wind. He
illustrated his views and the action of the bird in this way:

" Suppose the bird is gliding downward, without any flapping,
in calm air, and transforming a descent of 1 metre into 8
metres of forward progress. Now let us suppose the bird to
have an initial velocity of 1 kilometre per minute, say, 8 metres
in one half second; let the bird be immersed in a wind of 8
metres per half second, and blowing at right angles to its path.
Let us suppose, further, that this wind can elevate the bird 2
metres while it drifts it back 8 metres. Now the bird does not
want to rise, and must therefore expend the 2 metres of altitude. What does he do with it? He then transforms 1 metre
of potential altitude into 8 metres of progress against the wind
to overcome the drift which would otherwise result, and he
transforms also the remaining 1 metre of potential altitude into
8 metres of forward progress, with which he translates himself
in whatever direction he likes. Thus, as a final result, sailing
flight will afford him, after deducting all losses, a speed of 1
kilometre per minute."

It will be observed that the statement is not very clear, and that
there is no exact explanation as to how the feat is accomplished.
Most commentators have dismissed this explanation, together
with a somewhat similar statement made by the *Duke of Argyll*
in " The Reign of Law," with the remark that if it is meant to
imply that the bird alternately transforms altitude into speed,
part of which is lost in overcoming resistance, and transmutes
the reduced speed into a recovery of the original altitude, that
then this involves perpetual motion, and that the latter is an
absurdity.

*Mr. V. Tatin* is more specific in his criticism. In the course
of an article in the " *Revue Scientifique* " of Nov. 7, 1891, he
says:

" It seems to me that the error is apparent. If the bird first
progresses 8 metres by descending 1 metre, there is no reason
why the descent should not continue, and it is quite gratuitously
that *d'Esterno* adds: ' Suppose that the wind elevates the bird
2 metres.' This was easy to write, but why should the wind
elevate it 2 metres? We see clearly enough that it will be
drifted back 8 metres, because it must gradually acquire the
speed and direction of the surrounding medium, on which it

rests, but we see also that during this drift of 8 metres there will be descent, and not elevation.   This first prop being knocked away, all the remainder tumbles down."

This criticism is not quite fair, because it assumes that the bird will in the long run part with all his inertia.   He will not do so if he manages to extract energy from the wind, but the puzzle is to explain how he does it.   Almost all the observers have stated that it is accomplished by a skilful interchange of elevation for velocity and of velocity for elevation, but they are not agreed as to the explanation:

One of the most eminent of such observers was *M. Basté*. He published a carefully prepared paper (in French) in "*L'Aëronaute*" for September, October, and November, 1887, containing an excellent account of 40 selected typical observations made by himself from 1871 to 1885 upon the numerous sailing birds in Uruguay, the Argentine Republic, and Brazil. This paper is well worth studying by persons interested in the subject, and some of his diagrams of bird evolutions will be given herein farther on.

In his attempt at theoretical demonstration he assimilates the soaring bird to a kite, in which the string is replaced by weight, and he carries this theory farther than his predecessors, by showing that the uplift is quite sufficient to sustain the weight at the angles of incidence observed by himself, of 2° to 8°; but he fails to show how the forward propulsion is obtained, save by the inference that altitude and speed can be interchanged without loss.

For the uplift he adopts the formula, for angles of incidence between 1° and 7°, of:

$P = SP'\sin a$                                            in which ——— :

P = The lift on the bird.
P' = The air pressure due to the speed.
S = The sustaining surface of the bird.
Sin $a$ = The sine of the angle of incidence.

This formula gives materially less results than that of *Duchemin*, shown by *Professor Langley* to agree best with experiment in which the uplift is:

$$P = SP' \frac{2\sin a \cos a}{1 \quad \sin^2 a}$$

*Basté* applies his formula to two cases: the first, that of a gull weighing 0.64 pounds, and with 1.03 square feet surface (1.61 square feet per pound) exposed at an angle of 5° to a wind blowing at 44 miles per hour, and he calculates that the uplift is 0.99 pounds, or 50 per cent. more than the weight of the bird, so that it must rise. (This uplift would be 1.72 pounds by the Duchemin formula.) In the second case, he selects a falcon weighing 0.46 pound, with a surface of 1.28 square feet (2.78 square feet per pound) exposed at an angle of 12° to a wind of 20 miles per hour. His uplift amounts to 0.54 pounds, while it would be 0.99 pounds by the Duchemin formula.

*Basté* does not seem to have measured the wind when making his observations. The weak feature in his demonstration is that he has assumed winds of undue intensity, but this is offset by the fact that he has employed a formula which gives less than the real results. He says that with wing surfaces in the proportion of 2.69 to 2.93 square feet per pound birds can sail in winds of 4½ to 11 miles per hour; that birds with 1.46 to 1.71 square feet per pound require winds of 20 to 27 miles per hour, while birds with 1.37 to 1.46 square feet of wing surface per pound maintain and transport themselves in sailing flight in winds of 44 to 56 miles per hour.

This agrees fairly well with the observations of the present writer, which indicate that sailing flight is practicable to the buzzard weighing 0.88 pounds per square foot, in a 5 or 6 mile breeze, and to the gull weighing 1 pound per square foot, in a wind of 12 to 18 miles an hour.

*Basté*, however, does not show how the resistance of the body and wings is overcome, nor how the bird obtains forward motion. As a deduction he says:

" To resume the preceding observations and demonstrations I simply conclude: that sailing flight is the immediate result of a skilful combination of two forces possessing different intensity and direction, *i.e.*, the force of gravity and the pressure of an aerial current. But that, by reason of the faculty possessed by the bird, of changing the position of his body, of folding or inclining his wings, and of thereby displacing his centre of gravity, there results such a great diversity in the application of these two forces that the resulting movements become so complex as to constitute an entire system of aerial locomotion."

### 2.   RISING TRENDS OF WIND.

*Pénaud*, in an unfinished essay upon sailing flight in " *L'Aéronaute* " for March and April, 1875, accounted for the phenomenon by assuming ascending currents of wind to prevail,

and he adduced terrestrial slopes and obstacles, the impinging of wind currents upon each other, eddies and solar action, as abundant and adequate causes to produce such rising
winds.

Mathematically, this theory is quite satisfactory, even if we
base our calculations upon plane surfaces. If we assume, for
instance, an ascending trend inclined but 15° upward, and a
plane surface loaded to 1 pound to the square foot, and if we
suppose that surface to be inclined forwards, so that its front
edge shall point 5° *below* the horizon, then the wind will still
make an angle of 10° with the surface, at which angle the
normal pressure will be, by Duchemin's formula, 0.337 of what
it would be if the plane were at right angles to the wind. Now,
this normal pressure is decomposed into two resultants, the
" lift " and the " drift," which are as the cosine and the sine of
10° or angle of incidence. If next we suppose the wind to be
blowing at the rate of 25 miles per hour, at which the rectangular pressure, by ordinary wind tables, is 3.125 pounds per
square foot, we will then have for the lifting force :

Lift $= 1 \times 3.125 \times 0.337 \times \cos 10°$, or $0.985 = 1.03$ pounds,
which will a little more than sustain the weight. But the plane
is making an angle of 5° *below* the horizon, and the horizontal
component or " drift" is directed towards the front and acting
as a propelling force; we therefore have, with the same wind
pressure :

Drift $= 1 \times 3.125 \times 0.337 \times \sin 5°$, or $0.087 = 0.0916$
pounds, this being the propelling traction per square foot, so
that if the surface measures 1,000 square feet, it will be dragged
forward by a constant horizontal force of 91.6 pounds, and
this, inasmuch as the speed of the wind is 25 miles per hour,
amounts to :

$$\text{Power} = \frac{91.6 \times 25}{375} = 6.10 \text{ horse-power,}$$

which would enable the plane to advance horizontally against
this ascending wind, and to overcome the resistance of such
spars and body as might be requisite.

It will be seen hereafter that still better results can be figured
out by basing calculations upon the concave surfaces of birds'
wings.

This theory has been concurred in or separately advanced by
*De Louvrié, Moy, " Close Hauled,"* several other writers in the
technical press, and by *Lilienthal,* the latter stating that the

wind blowing over a level plain generally has an upward trend
of 3° or 4°, and that this is the principal reason for the sailing
flight of birds. It is very much to be regretted that he did not
publish his theory with full calculations.

The existence of ascending trends of wind is fully confirmed
by *Mr. Maxim* in an article entitled " Natural and Artificial
Flight," in the Aeronautical Annual for 1896. In this he describes his many observations at sea and on land, and deduces
the conclusion that the wind seldom or never blows in a horizontal direction, that there are ascending and descending columns
of air, generally separated from each other by distances varying from 500 feet to 20 miles, and that the soaring birds seek out
and utilize the ascending columns, being enabled to recognize
them through the sensitive air-cells which abound throughout
their bodies, and which act much as aneroid barometers.

This theory assimilates the soaring bird to a ship sailing close-
hauled upon the wind, the force of gravity replacing the effect
of the keel. Its defect is that it is not complete, for careful
observation shows that while local ascending trends of wind are
not uncommon, are indeed very frequent, yet the sailing birds
are sometimes seen to perform their feats perfectly when every
test shows the mean wind to be horizontal. I saw, for instance,
at Tampa, Florida, in February, 1893, three buzzards advance
half a mile dead against the wind, on a level course, without
one single flap, while the smoke from the tall chimney of the
adjoining hotel laundry, the top of which was about at the same
level as the birds, indicated that the wind was quite horizontal.

### 3. DIFFERENT COEFFICIENTS FRONT AND REAR OF BIRDS.

This theory approximates a bird circling in the sky to a set of
Robinson anemometer cups, which spin round and round by reason of the difference in coefficient of their concave and convex
sides. It was first advanced by *Mouillard* in " *L'Empire de
l'Air*," without, however, great insistance upon it. He held that
when the sailing bird went with the wind, the current exerted
pressure against the fluffy rear, so as to impart a speed which
was subsequently used in gaining height, when the bird presented his smooth front to the wind.

This conjecture was independently presented in 1894 by *Mr.
Winston*. It had also been advanced in 1884 by *M. Weyher*
in " *L'Aéronaute*," but the latter took it back in 1890, for the
very sound reason that the wind can in no case impart more than

its own speed to the bird, and that therefore the latter cannot, by turning around, then progress against the same wind.

*M. Mouillard* now holds the opinion that the soaring bird, having first acquired an initial speed of his own, either by flapping or by gliding downward, next receives impulse by heading into the wind, and is raised up, just as a car on a " roller coaster " would be lifted higher than its point of departure were the whole roadway to be set into motion in a contrary direction to the car, after the latter has begun running down the first incline.    His article setting forth this view will be found in the " Cosmopolitan Magazine " for February, 1894.

We next come to the fourth group of theories, which hold that energy is obtained by going over courses of differing lengths in:

### 4.  TACKING AND CIRCLING.

*Mr. S. E. Peal* has been carefully observing the soaring birds in Upper Assam, India, for many years.    He has repeatedly (much too briefly) published his observations, and in an article in "Nature," of May 21, 1891, which will well repay perusal, he brings out a number of important facts.    He states that Upper Assam is a dead level, some 60 miles wide by 200 long, that the prevailing wind is a steady breeze of about 5 to 10 miles an hour, that there are no up rushes of air, and that large birds like the cyrus, adjutant, pelican, and vulture can rise from 300 to 3,000 feet in a *steady* breeze without flapping their wings. He says:

" Firstly, these large birds do not soar in a dead calm or a storm, or during high winds.    They prefer a steady breeze.

" Secondly, they rise from the ground by flapping the wings, and continue this till they are 100 or 200 feet up, and then begin to soar, in right or left hand spirals 100 or 200 yards across.    At each lap they rise 10 or 20 feet, and make as many yards leeway, drifting slowly *with the wind*, and continue thus to rise until out of sight above. . . . The speed of the bird is always greater than the breeze, and the resistance is unequal on opposite sides of the loop of the spiral; least when it travels with the breeze, and greatest when on the opposite half, meeting it.

"It seems to me the solution is that when going with the wind the bird gathers momentum by going down a slight incline, and when it turns and meets the breeze, this extra momentum is used in lifting the bird and carrying it over a *shorter* course.

Thus it starts the next lap at a *slightly* higher level, but some 20 yards to leeward. Variation of the speed of the wind at different levels is here quite out of the question; the bird, too, keeps to its steady spiral, and as steadily ascends at each lap."

*Mr. Magnus Blum,* in a letter to " Nature," in February, 1891, modifies this theory by observing that when the bird, with an initial speed of its own, is sailing at right angles to the wind, he is also drifted sideways by the current; that hence he passes over the diagonal between those two courses, and does this in the same time that would otherwise be occupied by his own course in calm air; that as the diagonal is longer, the speed must be greater, the increment of velocity being gained from the wind, thus constituting the method by which the bird gathers the energy required to overcome the head resistance and to maintain the altitude, with, however, some oscillations in level when going with the wind or against it. Hence he infers that the fundamental evolution for the bird to perform consists in a series of zigzags, with loops at the turning points, and that spiral sailing is but a modification of this fundamental manœuvre. He gives no quantitative calculations to show that the impulse received is sufficient to overcome the head resistance and to maintain the velocity. We shall again find this zigzag or tacking idea, differently applied, in M. Bretonnière's paper, and it would seem worthy of closer investigation than it has yet received.

*Mr. Goupil,* in his book " *La Locomotion Aérienne,*" advances substantially the same idea (page 69), that the bird gathers energy from the wind when sailing quartering, or at right angles thereto; but he gives no calculations to show that the effect is sufficient to account for the phenomenon.

*Professor Proctor* evidently inclined to the general explanation offered by Peal, but did not exactly formulate a theory. He wrote quite a number of interesting short articles on the subject. One of them, a letter to the " English Mechanic," occasioned a lively controversy by a dozen writers, which was republished in the report of the Aeronautical Society of Great Britain for 1880. Although somewhat inconclusive, it is worth perusal by the curious.

*Prince Mikounine* made some interesting observations upon the soaring flight of vultures in the mountains of the Caucasus, which he published in " *L'Aéronaute* " for September, 1878. He endeavored to place himself on the same level as the birds, and carefully noted the direction of the wind. He alone, of all

the various observers, thought that the birds rose when going
with the wind, and descended when facing it.

## 5.  COMBINATION OF GRAVITY AND WIND.

*M. S. Drzewiecki*, a Russian engineer, who presented a
very able paper in French at the Aeronautical Congress at
Paris in 1889, upon "Birds considered as Animated Aeroplanes," followed this up in 1891 with an essay upon "Soaring
Flight," which was printed for private circulation.

In the exposition of his theory he supposes a bird, on a
perch and facing the wind, to glide downward and forward
against the breeze, so that the two velocities shall combine.
He shows that by bringing his centre of gravity forward the
bird will descend, and, calling V his potential speed, g the factor for gravity, and h the height, then the velocity due to the
fall will be: $V = \sqrt{2\,gh}$.  He then goes on to say: "Hence
the bird, at the lowest point in its course, will possess this absolute speed V (as regards the earth); then by a fresh displacement of his centre of gravity, the inverse of that at starting, he
will alter his angle of incidence so as to transform his descent,
first into horizontal translation and then into a progressive rise,
against the wind as before.  At the time of the transformation
of the descent into a horizontal movement, the absolute speed
V, that due to the fall, being combined against the velocity $-\,V'$
of the wind, which is blowing adversely, will give the bird a relative velocity against the air of $V + V'$.

"Hence, like a child's marble rolled against an inclined plane
which is made to travel in a contrary direction, the bird will
rise to a greater height than its starting point, or to an altitude
depending upon his relative speed of $V + V'$ of:

$$\frac{(V + V')^2}{2g}.$$

"But if, instead of availing of all this potential lift the bird,
through a new change in his angle of incidence, ceases to rise
at a point where the remaining speed will still be equal to $V'$,
and hence be sufficient to uplift him to the height

$$\frac{V'^2}{2g},$$

it is evident that the difference in altitude between the lowest
point reached and that last mentioned will be:

$$h' = \frac{(V+V')^2}{2g} - \frac{V'^2}{2g},$$

and, in consequence thereof, the bird will have arisen from the lowest point:

$$h' = \frac{V^2 + 2\,VV'}{2g},$$

and will still possess a speed of V′ relative to the air. This velocity being equal to that of the wind, it follows that the bird is then under precisely the same conditions (except that he is free in air) as when he was on the perch before starting, and is ready for another descent.

"In the first descent the bird lost in altitude

$$h = \frac{V^2}{2g};$$

he regained, as we have already seen,

$$h' = \frac{V^2 + 2VV'}{2g},$$

and hence the altitude gained by the evolution was

$$H = h' - h = \frac{2VV'}{2g}.$$

"Upon the next evolution the soaring bird will continue to gain altitude, and can thus rise indefinitely without muscular effort, by profiting exclusively of the speed of the wind."

M. Drzewiecki then describes the two methods which may be practised by the bird in effecting this recuperative descent; 1st, by progressively changing his angle of incidence, so as to keep his longitudinal axis always tangent to his trajectory, and 2d, by maintaining constantly his aeroplane at the angle of least resistance, which M. Drzewiecki finds to be 1° 50′ 45″. He holds that the first method is adopted when the wind's speed is greater than that of the bird, and the second method obtains when it is less.

He then applies these principles to helical circling in the air, which he considers as the fundamental manœuvre, and he estimates that once altitude is gained, the bird can glide downward in the same direction as the wind at an angle of 2° 31′ 10″, or in the ratio of 45 horizontal feet for every foot of descent.

The objection to this theory, as expounded, is that the speed due to gravity v is a *vertical* speed, and that the speed of the wind v′ being a *horizontal* speed they should not be added

together.   The true *relative* speed would seem to be the diagonal of the parallelogram of velocities, or $\sqrt{v^2 + v'^2}$, instead of
v + v′; but, on the other hand, this "relative wind" will not be
horizontal, as assumed by *M. Drzewiecki;* it will be inclined
upward as regards the course of the bird, and thus perform the
office of a rising trend of wind.

Some loss would seem to be involved in the supposing the
bird to leave the perch dead against the wind, and accordingly
*M. Bretonnière*, in a paper on "Sailing Flight" presented to the
International Conference on Aerial Navigation at Chicago in
1893, modifies the theory by considering the bird as leaving
the perch on a course at right angles to the wind, and then,
drifting a little, descending so as to gain speed from gravity,
which speed is thereafter transformed into elevation by heading
into the wind.   The mathematical demonstration is practically
the same as that of *M. Drzewiecki*, the vertical and horizontal
speeds being added together; but, according to *M. Bretonnière*,
the fundamental manœuvre is a zigzag instead of a circular
sweep, and he holds that this would be the proper manœuvre
for a man to perform if he were attempting to imitate the
soaring birds.

Unfortunately neither of these writers has explained how the
bird extracts energy from the wind, and *Mr. Soreau*, a French
engineer, in an article in the "*Revue Scientifique*" for March
30 and April 6, 1895, criticises them as follows:

"The conclusion in M. Bretonnière's theory is quite erroneous.   .   .   .   A uniform wind is impotent in the mechanics
of flight; its variations alone can benefit the birds.   .   .   .   In
the theory of *M. Drzewiecki* the author says naught concerning
ascending currents or wind squalls, and yet he talks of work
obtained from the wind.   He attempts to demonstrate that the
bird, by gathering increased speed through gravity, can then
rise higher than he fell.   In such case, the transformation into
height of the kinetic energy due to the fall would be greater
than the original unit!   It is just the reverse of what really
occurs."

*Mr. A. M. Wellington*, in a paper on "Mechanics of Flight"
presented at the same conference, held that the soaring bird
gathered speed from the wind by plunging downward in the
same direction in which it blows, and he likens the action to
that of a spherical mass rolling down an inclined plane on a
floating hulk which travels in the same direction as the rolling
ball.   As in this case the ball would be travelling faster than

the hulk, it is difficult to see how'it could gather energy there-from, although it would doubtless gather speed and energy from gravity, which would send it up again, barring losses, to the same height it started from.

It will be noted that all these theories are based upon the assumption that what we call the "wind" blows as a practically uniform current of air, regular both in velocity and direction.

Many eminent scientists hold, however, that for the sailing bird a uniform current is equivalent to a calm, and they brush aside all the above theories except Pénaud's, upon the ground that it is not physically possible for sailing flight to occur in a uniform current.

*Lord Rayleigh*, the highest scientific authority in Great Britain, says in an interesting letter published in "Nature," April 5, 1883:

"I premise that if we know anything about mechanics, it is certain that a bird, without working his wings, cannot, either in still air or in a uniform horizontal wind, maintain his level indefinitely. For a short time such maintenance is possible at the expense of an initial relative velocity, but this must soon be exhausted. Whenever, therefore, a bird pursues his course for some time without working his wings, we must conclude either (1) that the course is not horizontal, (2) that the wind is not horizontal, or (3) that the wind is not uniform. It is probable that the truth is usually represented by (1) or (2); but the question I wish to raise is whether the cause suggested by (3) may not sometimes come into operation."

*Lord Rayleigh* then states that circular sailing is possible without flapping if the wind be stratified into two layers of different velocities, for by keeping near the plane of separation, the bird can gain relative velocity without work in passing from one stratum to the other; but he adds that, *à priori*, he would not have supposed that the variation of velocity of the wind, as the height increases, would be adequate for the purpose of sailing flight.

This brings us to the three groups of theories which suppose energy to be derived by the bird from irregularities in the wind.

## 6.  DIFFERENT SPEEDS OF WIND STRATA.

One of the best expositions of this theory is that of *Mr. Wm. Kress* in a paper entitled "A Theory of Sailing Flight," read before the Conference on Aerial Navigation of 1893. He supposes the moving sea of air to be composed of strata of wind of different speeds, vertically superposed. He shows by a table that a circling bird in passing from a current blowing 5 metres per second (11 miles per hour) into another of 10 metres per second (22 miles per hour) can be at all times supported without beating his wings, and can then return into the original current with a velocity increased by 3 metres per second.

It is well known that winds do almost invariably increase in speed with altitude, but the cases must be rare indeed in which the increase is as great as *Mr. Kress* has assumed within the limits of one of the bird's circlings; so that although the theory itself is sound, it remains to be proved that the exact variations assumed exist in nature.

*Mr. H. C. Vogt*, of Copenhagen, in a letter to London "Engineering," published March 25, 1892, gave a series of elaborate computations to show that an albatross weighing 20 pounds, with 11 square feet of sustaining surface, derives from a stratified wind all the necessary energy to sustain his weight and to advance against that wind. For this purpose he supposes the gale to blow at the rate of 60 feet per second (41 miles an hour) at a height of 65 feet over the sea level, and of 30 feet per second just over the wave tops. The bird is assumed to commence his manœuvres at a height of 65 feet over the sea, to descend to the calmer region at the sea level, gathering 1,410 foot-pounds of energy, and to reascend against the wind to his original altitude of 65 feet, having advanced against the wind a distance of 250 feet in 6.25 seconds, and being then ready to repeat the operation. This letter should be carefully read by all interested in the question. The calculations are correct, and it is not impossible that in a 40-mile gale and a rolling sea there should be as great differences as those assumed in the speed of the wind aloft and at the sea level, but the computations only apply to this special case, and do not explain how a hawk or a buzzard can sail indefinitely on pulseless wings in a breeze of 5 or 6 miles per hour.

## 7. INTERMITTENCY OF WIND FORCE.

The difficulty in conceiving how a bird could extract energy from a uniform current of wind led *Professor Marey*, in his masterly book "*Le Vol des Oiseaux*," published in 1889, to suggest that sailing flight might be accounted for by the intermittency in wind velocities which are known to exist. He showed that it was quite possible for a bird to be sustained, to advance against the wind, and to rise, without flapping, if it could avail of a series of wind gusts and relative calms occurring at appropriate intervals. This he illustrated by a figure (page 316) somewhat similar to that which will be hereinafter given in discussing the manœuvre of the gull rising from a pile-head, but he did not elaborate this theory, nor show just what fluctuations occurred in the wind.

It was reserved for *Professor Langley* to set forth this theory fully in his now celebrated essay on "The Internal Work of the Wind." He showed by records of instrumental measurements, ingeniously made so as to give the actual facts, that the wind is very far from being a uniform current, such, for instance, as a stream of water; that, in fact, the wind is constantly fluctuating in velocity and force, not only in those gusts and comparative calms which are apparent to our senses, but in numberless minor fluctuations which had not previously been revealed, in consequence of the inertia of the measuring instruments employed. *Professor Langley* then showed that it is quite possible to conceive how a sailing bird can maintain himself in the air, and also advance against the wind without work, by taking advantage of these fluctuations. This it can do by merely altering its balance and consequent angle of incidence. By increasing this angle during a wind gust the bird can gain altitude, and by diminishing this angle during a lull he can glide downward and gather velocity, to be subsequently expended in regaining altitude. This is illustrated by a figure drawn from theoretical considerations alone, which is almost identical with the figure to be hereinafter given from actual measurements of the gull starting from the pile-head.

This paper will, of course, be read in full by all interested in the subject. It has been published by the Smithsonian Institution and in the "Proceedings of the International Conference on Aerial Navigation," and need not therefore be further epitomized here.

The theory is entirely sound, but not quite complete. There is no question in my own mind but that sailing birds do utilize prolonged wind gusts in gaining altitude, and do gain velocity during relative calms by gliding downward, but I question whether they can utilize the minor fluctuations of the wind, especially in light breezes, and whether the wind gusts and relative calms are sufficiently timely and strong to account for spiral soaring. The author of this theory has yet to show by quantitative calculations that the fluctuations of the wind, as actually observed, are sufficient to produce the required support and advance of a sailing bird weighing, say, 1 pound per square foot of sustaining surface, and how the various manœuvres and feats of soaring flight which have been observed are to be accounted for.

It may be mentioned here as a curious illustration how similar conclusions are simultaneously reached by able thinkers, that only a few months prior to the presentation of Professor Langley's essay, the same identical theory was briefly propounded by *Mr. W. H. Dines*, the eminent British meteorologist, in a private letter to myself, and that I subsequently found a somewhat similar theory, evidently quite original, in an Italian book, "*Teoria del Volo*," by A. Faccioli, published by U. Hoepli, Milan, in 1895.

### 8. CHANGES IN WIND DIRECTION.

The suggestion of *Lord Rayleigh*, that among the three inferences which may be drawn in accounting for sailing flight is " that the wind is not uniform," covers, of course, changes in direction as well as in velocity. *Professor Langley* mentions that changes in direction of wind occurred during his experiments, although they were not recorded by his instruments. By such changes in direction, both vertical and horizontal, *Prof. A. L. Zahm*, then of Notre Dame University, accounted for what he termed " Naval Soaring," in an article published in the "*Notre Dame Scholastic*" of Dec. 10, 1892.

This theory assimilates sailing flight to the tacking of a ship, gravity and inertia answering for keel resistance. It explains the zigzags and the circlings which soaring birds so frequently exhibit, and is a sound explanation provided the changes in direction can be shown to obtain with sufficient force and frequency to produce the observed manœuvres. To determine this, *Professor Zahm* subsequently constructed an experimental apparatus to record simultaneously the changes in vertical and horizontal direction which occur in the wind. He has published the results in a paper entitled " Atmospheric Gusts and their Relation to Flight," which will be found in the " Proceedings of the International Conference in Aerial Navigation." The experimental apparatus not proving quite satisfactory, he has not attempted to apply its records to quantitative calculations in support of his theory, but it is to be hoped that he

shall soon find time to resume this interesting investigation, as it
showed greater variations in wind direction than is generally
realized by our unaided senses.

From my recent experiments with full-sized gliding machines,
carrying a man, I am now inclined to attribute the fluctuations
in wind velocities observed by *Professor Langley*, and those in
wind direction observed by *Professor Zahm*, largely to one and
the same cause. This is the apparently rotary or oscillating
character of wind currents. To the man in the machine,
buffeted by the wind, the current seemed to arrive as a series of
revolving billows, and to veer in direction and in velocity according to the position which the apparatus might occupy at any
one time with reference to the centre of rotation of the aerial
wave. This observation was originally due to *Mr. A. M.
Herring*, who most frequently used the various machines
experimented with, and once the fact was pointed out all the
subsequent observations seemed to confirm the idea that all
wind waves have a more or less rolling character. The reader
needs but to watch smoke issuing from a chimney, to gain an
impression as to the shape of these wind waves, and to conceive
the changes in velocity and direction which will be experienced
by a stationary object exposed thereto, or by a sailing bird
passing through them. It is believed that, as it has practically
no inertia, the smoke immediately partakes in a large measure
of the motion of the air, and that its curlings represent the
conditions which must be met in free flight. This observation
is of important promise, as furnishing a better understanding
of the character of the wind, and as suggesting what to investigate in further attempts to imitate the birds.

Having now passed in review all the theories of sailing
flight of which the writer hereof has knowledge, the reader will
note that none of them takes into account the shape of the birds
themselves, and that no mention seems to have been made of
the cross-sections of the wings of sailing or other birds. If
these various theories were true and complete it would follow
*that all birds could soar*, and yet it is well known that the great
majority of birds, even those of considerable mass, such as the
geese, the ducks, the wild turkeys, etc., can glide a limited
distance, but that they cannot sail upon the wind like the eagles,
the vultures, the gulls, or the albatrosses. In fact, sailing flight is
confined to a few species, and the performance is chiefly seen
in particular localities.

This led the writer hereof to question whether there might

not be some important difference in the cross-section of the wings of soaring and non-soaring birds, and a brief investigation revealed such divergences as to lead to the inference that this difference in shape may alone account for the fact that one class of birds can extract energy from the wind while other classes cannot.

These differences are fairly shown in Fig. 1, which represents the cross-section of the wings of the frigate, the buzzard, the gray pelican, the gull, and the hawk, all of them soaring birds, and of the duck, the pigeon, and the wild turkey, which are non-soarers. These sections are all taken just forward of the first joint in the arm, and exhibit a marked difference between the sailing and the non-sailing birds. It will be noticed that the former have all a downward projecting lobe at the front, and that the radius of curvature at about one-quarter of the distance back from the front edge is considerably sharper on the under side than on the upper side of the wing, while the non-soarers have not only thinner wings, but the curvature is nearly the same on the upper and the lower surfaces. It is probable that all these wings are somewhat flatter than here shown when in full action carrying weight, but all the sailing and non-sailing birds which I have examined exhibit the same kind of difference in shape, and I believe that it will be found universal. The inference which I have drawn therefrom will be stated when we come to discuss what has been called "aspiration."

One other matter of observation has also greatly impressed me. It is the fact that sailing flight seems to be most frequently and easily performed in the regions of more uniform air currents: in the steady trade winds, in the regular sea breezes, and in those southern zephyrs in which it is hard to detect sufficient fluctuations in velocity to produce the effects which have been theoretically ascribed to them.

And yet there is nothing more certain than that the sailing birds extract energy from such winds; that buzzards, for instance, maintain themselves in the air at speeds of 15 to 20 miles per hour without a flap of wing, in breezes of 6 to 8 miles an hour; that gulls can keep up indefinitely at speeds of 17 to 22 miles per hour, in winds of 13 to 16 miles per hour, and that the fluctuations of these winds, either in velocity or direction, do not seem to be great. Indeed, it has not infrequently occurred to me that the sailing birds seemed to dislike gusty winds, and that they aided themselves by flapping more often in such winds than they did in steady breezes.

These facts led me to question whether it was not possible that sailing flight might take place in a nearly uniform wind; but, as previously stated, it was only when I obtained Herr Lilienthal's table of air pressures, published in Moedebeck's "Handbook for Aeronauts and Aviators," that I was enabled to figure out satisfactory reactions at the angles and speeds which I had observed.

This table is understood to have been obtained from actual experiments with surfaces arched upward (in section) about $\frac{1}{12}$ of their width, and in presenting it *Herr Lilienthal* (using metric units) says:

"When a wing with an arched profile is struck by the wind at an angle *a* with a velocity V, there will be generated an air pressure R which generally is not normal to the chord, but is the resultant of a force N normal to the chord, and of another force T tangential to the chord. If we call F the area of the wing, then:

* The normal pressure $N = \eta \times 0.13 \times F \times V^2$.
* The tangential pressure $T = \vartheta \times 0.13 \times F \times V^2$.

"The table on the following page, giving values of $\eta$ and $\vartheta$, show that arched surfaces still possess supporting powers when they are struck by the air at an acute angle *from above*, that is to say when *a* becomes negative. The resisting components of the air pressure T change, with angles exceeding 3°, into propelling components, which, at an angle of 15°, become equal to $\frac{1}{12}$ of the lift, and do not disappear entirely until 30° is reached."

This does not mean, as *Lilienthal* subsequently makes clear by an example, that there is no horizontal component of the *normal pressure* N, or "drift," when the angle of incidence is above the horizon, but that, at certain angles, the *tangential pressure* T, which would be parallel with the surface if applied to a plane, and therefore produce no effect but friction, acts on a curved surface as a propelling force.

This table, which will be used in the calculations hereinafter given, is as follows:

---

* 0.13 × F × V² in metric units = 0.005 × S × V² in miles per hour.

TABLE OF NORMAL AND TANGENTIAL PRESSURES

Deduced by Lilienthal from the diagrams on Plate VI., in his book "Bird-flight as the Basis of the Flying Art."

| $a$ Angle. | $\eta$ Normal. | $\vartheta$ Tangential. | $a$ Angle. | $\eta$ Normal. | $\vartheta$ Tangential. |
|---|---|---|---|---|---|
| — 9° ....... | 0.000 | + 0.070 | 16° ........ | 0.909 | — 0.075 |
| — 8° ....... | 0.040 | + 0.067 | 17° ........ | 0.915 | — 0.073 |
| — 7° ....... | 0.080 | + 0.064 | 18° ........ | 0.919 | — 0.070 |
| — 6° ....... | 0.120 | + 0.060 | 19° ........ | 0.921 | — 0.065 |
| — 5° ....... | 0.160 | + 0.055 | 20° ........ | 0.922 | — 0.059 |
| — 4° ....... | 0.200 | + 0.049 | 21° ........ | 0.923 | — 0.053 |
| — 3° ....... | 0.242 | + 0.043 | 22° ........ | 0.924 | — 0.047 |
| — 2° ....... | 0.286 | + 0.037 | 23° ........ | 0.924 | — 0.041 |
| — 1° ....... | 0.332 | + 0.031 | 24° ........ | 0.923 | — 0.036 |
| 0° ....... | 0.381 | + 0.024 | 25° ........ | 0.922 | — 0.031 |
| + 1° ....... | 0.434 | + 0.016 | 26° ........ | 0.920 | — 0.026 |
| + 2° ....... | 0.489 | + 0.008 | 27° ........ | 0.918 | — 0.021 |
| + 3° ....... | 0.546 | 0.000 | 28° ........ | 0.915 | — 0.016 |
| + 4° ....... | 0.600 | — 0.007 | 29° ........ | 0.912 | — 0.012 |
| + 5° ....... | 0.650 | — 0.014 | 30° ........ | 0.910 | — 0.008 |
| + 6° ....... | 0.696 | — 0.021 | 32° ........ | 0.906 | 0.000 |
| + 7° ....... | 0.737 | — 0.028 | 35° ........ | 0.896 | + 0.010 |
| + 8° ....... | 0.771 | — 0.035 | 40° ........ | 0.890 | + 0.016 |
| + 9° ....... | 0.800 | — 0.042 | 45° ........ | 0.888 | + 0.020 |
| 10° ...... | 0.825 | — 0.050 | 50° ........ | 0.888 | + 0.023 |
| 11° ...... | 0.846 | — 0.058 | 55° ........ | 0.890 | + 0.026 |
| 12° ...... | 0.864 | — 0.064 | 60° ........ | 0.900 | + 0.028 |
| 13° ...... | 0.879 | — 0.070 | 70° ........ | 0.930 | + 0.030 |
| 14° ...... | 0.891 | — 0.074 | 80° ........ | 0.960 | + 0.015 |
| 15° ...... | 0.901 | — 0.076 | 90° ........ | 1.000 | 0.000 |

While I feel quite certain that most of the sailing feats which have so puzzled observers are performed in consequence of ascending trends of wind, or by the aid of wind gusts, lulls, and changes of direction, — that, in fact, sailing birds do constantly utilize such trends and fluctuations, — I am also constrained to believe, from many personal observations, that the theories above reviewed are not complete, and that birds of certain types do extract energy from a wind which all visible tests show to be horizontal, and blowing with such slight fluctuations that the required reactions cannot, with our present knowledge, be figured out from the observed facts.

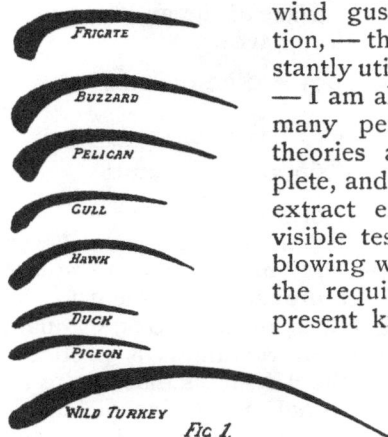

FRIGATE

BUZZARD

PELICAN

GULL

HAWK

DUCK

PIGEON

WILD TURKEY

FIG. 1.

I believe that this possible obtaining of energy in such cases is due to the section of wing peculiar to sailing birds, as shown in figure 1; but before attempting the consideration of this, it seems best to consider more obvious cases, and to begin with the manœuvre of the gulls patrolling along the weather side of a steamer tied to the wharf.

The average measured velocity of the wind on that occasion was 12.78 miles per hour, it had an ascending trend of 10° to 20° at the side of the steamer, and the relative speed of the birds was 26.3 feet per second, or 17.88 miles per hour. They presented an angle of incidence of 5° to 7° *above the horizon.*

I found it impossible to compute the forces in action with the Duchemin formula for pressures on planes, even with a coefficient of 1.30 for the concavity of the supporting surfaces (obtained from some rough experiments with a pigeon — a non-soaring bird). An inadequate *sustaining* reaction could be figured out, but the *propulsion* could not be accounted for. If the angle of incidence had been negative a propelling force could have been calculated even for a plane, but as the observations showed that the angle was positive the whole case was dropped. Three years later, however, the Lilienthal coefficients rendered the matter easy of explanation.

As the relative speed of the bird was 17.88 miles an hour, it corresponded to a rectangular pressure of 1.60 pounds per square foot. Taking the lowest observed angles of incidence or 5° above the horizon for the bird, and 10° of ascending trend for the wind, the two would make an angle of 15° with each other, for which the Lilienthal coefficient for normal pressure is 0.901. The supporting surface of the gull measured was 2.015 square feet, and we therefore have:

$$\text{Normal} = 2.015 \times 1.60 \times 0.901 = 2.90 \text{ pounds.}$$

But as the angle of application is 15°, we have:

$$\text{Lift} = 2.90 \times \cos 15°, \text{ or } 0.966 = 2.80 \text{ pounds,}$$

which more than sustains the weight of 2.188 pounds.

The resistances consist in the "drift" and the resistance offered by the body and wing edges. The body measures 0.126 square feet in cross-section, and the most probable coefficient for its "fair" shape is 1/10. The wing edges measure 0.098 square feet in section, and their coefficient for roundness is probably 1/4. The course being horizontal, the "drift" is that due to an angle of +5°, for which the Lilienthal normal coefficient is 0.650. This factor must be multiplied by the sine of +5°; that is, by 0.087. We then have:

Drift = 2.015 × 1.60 × 0.65 × 0.087 =  0.182 pounds.
Body resistance = 0.126 × 1.60 ÷ 10 = 0.020    "
Wing resistance = 0.098 × 1.60 ÷ 4 =  0.039    "
                                      _____
        Total resistance,            0.241    "

But the tangential pressure is that due to 15°, the angle between the bird and the ascending wind, and for this the Lilienthal coefficient is — 0.076, so that the propelling factor is:

Tangential pressure = 2.015 × 1.60 × — 0.076 = — 0.245 pounds;

whence it appears that the resistances and the propulsion are practically equal, and that the bird can continue his patrol indefinitely without beat of wing, as he derives all the energy needed for this purpose from the ascending wind. As the speed is 26.3 feet per second the work so done is:

$$\text{Energy} = 0.245 \times 26.3 = 6.44 \text{ foot-pounds per second.}$$

This amounts to 0.0053 horse-power per pound of bird, equivalent to 188 pounds sustained per horse-power. It well illustrates the superiority of arched surfaces over planes, for it will be recollected that in figuring out the propulsion of 1,000 pounds on as many square feet, 6.10 horse-power was required to overcome the "drift" of the plane alone, without allowing for body or wing edge resistance, and we had to assume in sailing flight a negative angle of 5° for the plane and an ascending wind of 15°, blowing at 25 miles per hour, as against an ascending trend of 10°, blowing at 12.78 miles an hour on an arched surface, as just above calculated.

The sailing of the gulls just above and to the leeward of the coal pockets is probably to be accounted for in the same way, *i.e.*, by an ascending local current in a breeze too light to furnish support and propulsion if horizontal, for when the breeze grew stronger the birds soared all over the harbor in apparently horizontal winds. Unfortunately they were then at so great a height that the angle of incidence could not be seen. This angle was, however, fairly well observed during flapping flight in calm air, and was judged to be from 3° to 5° above the horizon. Assuming the first figure, and the lowest observed speed of 30 feet per second, or 20.4 miles an hour, for which the rectangular pressure is 2.08 pounds per square foot, we have, using the Lilienthal coefficients:

Normal = 2.015 × 2.08 × 0.546 = 2.288 pounds,
And lift = 2.288 × cos 3°, or 0.998 = 2.283 pounds,

which is seen to sustain the weight; while we have:

Drift = 2.288 × sin. 3°, or 0.052 = 0.119 pounds.
Body = 0.126 × 2.08 ÷ 10 =        0.026   "
Wings = 0.098 × 2.08 ÷ 4 =        0.051   "
                                 _____
Total resistance,                 0.196   "
Tangential pressure at 3°,        0.000   "

Work = 0.196 × 30 = 5.88 foot-pounds per second, or 0.0049 horse-power per pound of bird, which power, however, is furnished by the bird instead of being derived from the wind.

A manœuvre much more difficult to account for is that of the gull starting from a pile head (described under the head of "Starting"), and gaining a limited increase of altitude while advancing against the wind. There is no question as to the accuracy of the observation. The feat, although rare, was repeatedly witnessed by myself as well as by others. The bird, after rising without beat of wing 2 or 3 feet, descended about 8½ or 9 feet, then rose again some 12 feet, or say 3 to 3½ feet above the point at which he came to a poise, as shown in figure 2.

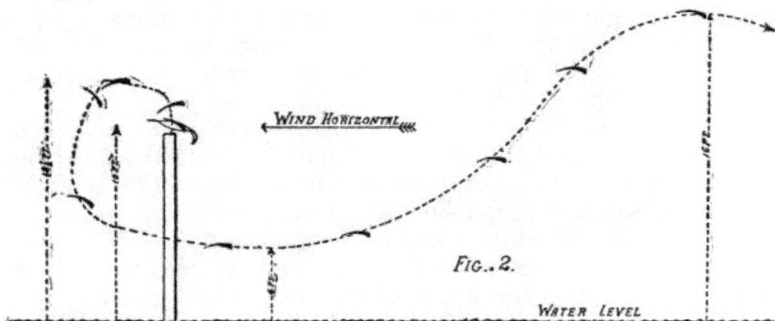

*Wind Horizontal*

*Fig. 2.*

*Water Level*

The bird was 10 feet above the water, facing a wind which I am sure was horizontal and varying from 14 to 23 feet per second, or 9.52 to 15.64 miles per hour. These speeds were measured by a " Richards " anemometer, but as the observations lasted from 10 to 20 seconds each, it is probable that neither the maximum nor the minimum was recorded. A detailed analysis of the subsequent performance will show that it can be accounted for by a variety of suppositions.

The gull first opened his wings wide, but as he kept the front edge depressed, the wind blew on his back and pressed him downward. Then, when a wind gust arrived, he raised the front edges to an angle of incidence estimated at 20° above the horizon, and rose upward. Let us assume that the gust blew at the rate of 18 miles an hour, or a very little more than the average maximum observed. According to ordinary tables of wind pressures, the speed assumed corresponds to a pressure of 1.62 pounds per square foot. Then, as the bird's sustaining area was 2.015 square feet and the Lilienthal coefficient is 0.922 for 20°, we have :

Normal = 2.015 × 1.62 × 0.922 = 3.01 pounds.

And as the angle is 20°, cosine 0.939, therefore :

Lift = 3.01 × 0.939 = 2.826 pounds.

As the bird's weight was 2.188 pounds, he needs must rise; but as the angle is above the horizon, the "drift" is positive, and the negative tangential pressure being small in comparison, he must needs also drift backward, thus losing relative speed and inertia. He will, theoretically, come to a poise when the lift just equals his weight. At 20° of incidence this will occur when the relative velocity becomes 15.87 miles per hour, corresponding to a rectangular pressure of 1.26 pounds per square foot. We then have:

$$\text{Lift} = 2.015 \times 1.26 \times 0.922 \times 0.939 = 2.188 \text{ pounds.}$$

It will appear by examination of theoretical tables of potential lifts against gravity, due to a given velocity of motion, that a speed of 18 miles per hour corresponds to a fall (or lift) of 10.84 feet, while a speed of 15.87 miles per hour corresponds to a fall of 8.63 feet; so that the gull could theoretically rise 10.84 —8.63 or 2.22 feet without the aid of the upward jump which he usually makes, but would lose 2.13 miles per hour of his relative speed. This agrees closely with the observed rise of 2 to 3 feet.

He could, however, go no higher with the wind then prevailing. He therefore altered his angle of incidence, by simply thrusting his wings back, thereby causing the weight of his body to tilt him to a negative angle of incidence as he plunged downward.

The problem to solve is how he subsequently gathers energy from the horizontal wind.

It is clear that if at the precise moment that the bird came to a poise the wind lulled materially, although this might be less than to the observed minimum of 9.52 miles per hour, the gull would acquire vertical speed more quickly than otherwise, and that if a fresh gust occurred just as he reached the lowest point of his course, he would again have been benefited by an increased relative velocity. This is the theory set forth by *Professor Langley*.

It is also clear that if the wind arrives as a billow revolving on a horizontal axis, and the bird starts up from the pile head on its ascending trend, and comes to a poise on its crest, he will be benefited by being able to gain speed upon the downward trend. The wind, upon the occasions when this performance was exhibited, blew at a speed varying from 14 to 23 feet per second, so that if those extremes had occurred during any single wave, they would have indicated a speed of rotation of

4.5 feet per second, this being one-half of the difference between the extremes recorded, while the mean velocity is 18.5 feet per second.  If the speed of rotation be 4.5 feet, and the horizontal velocity 18.5 feet per second, then we have an ascending trend of $\frac{4.5}{18.5} = 0.243 = 14°$, which we have already seen to be ample to furnish the required propelling power.

As many times, however, as I watched this manœuvre, the course gone over seemed to be identically the same : the gulls never failed to rise some 2 or 3 feet, to descend to within about 4 feet of the water, nor to rise thence about 12 feet, and, although there is a certain synchronism about the rotating billows, it seems difficult to believe, in the absence of actual measurements which I have not taken, that the rolling aerial waves, or the gusts and the lulls, occurred with such absolute exactness as to serve the bird at the very instant when he came to a poise because the relative velocity no longer sufficed to keep him up, so as to enable him to descend in a comparative calm, and to meet with another wave or gust at the exact time when he arrived at the bottom of his course.

There is another way in which the bird may gather energy from the wind during his descent at a negative angle to the horizon.   When he first plunges downward, *the wind blows on his back*, and thus accelerates his fall to a greater speed than that due to gravity alone, and this increased speed can thereafter be transformed into greater elevation.   This action, however, can continue but a very brief period, because it will drift the bird still further back, and because, as soon as he begins to fall, pressure accumulates under his wings, and he gradually flattens his angle of incidence.   I have made a number of computations of the foot-pounds which can be so gained, based upon a number of assumptions of the coefficient of air pressure due to the convexity of the bird's back, the varying angle of incidence, and the length of time of the action, but they do not fully account for the subsequent rise of 3.5 feet above the point where he came to his first poise, and I freely confess that I am unable to show how the bird gathers energy from the wind, save on the assumption of an opportune gust.

Moreover, this only applies to one particular manœuvre, which is rarely seen, and which may be accounted for by the existence of exceptional circumstances, like some of the soaring feats described by *Basté*.   One of these he terms the "Planement sur place," which may be rendered as soaring on a vertical stand, as shown in section in figure 3.  The bird was high in air, facing a strong wind at M, with an angle of incidence above the horizon. He was then seen to ascend on rigid wings, drifting backward through positions 2 and 3, until he arrived at M', position 4, whence he descended and advanced through positions 5, 6, and 7, until he once more reached the point M.

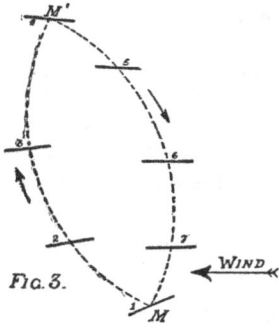

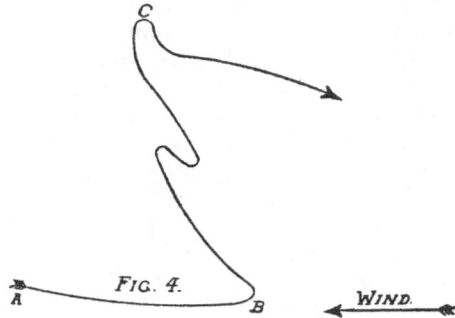

It seems reasonable to believe that in this case the bird simply utilized a wind gust to rise, coming to a poise at M' when the lull began, and thence descended by gravity. The gust may or may not have had an ascending trend. There does not seem to be much doubt that there was an ascending trend, however, during another feat described by *Basté*, which was also performed during a very high wind, and which is shown in vertical section in figure 4. The bird was at A, about 10 feet above the sea, and first glided against the wind to B, whence he rose some 150 feet to C, with a poise and a short downward plunge about the middle of the course. *Basté* draws the wind as horizontal, but the manœuvre indicates an intermittent gust with a rising trend, during which the bird gained much altitude which might be subsequently utilized in gliding.

Such feats, although very interesting in themselves, are easily accounted for by the exceptional circumstances under which they are performed; but the explanation does not account for the continuous sailing of birds on set wings in breezes so light that some observers have claimed that the evolutions take place in a dead calm. I have myself seen a buzzard sailing 75 feet overhead in a breeze which measured 1½ miles per hour at a height of 5 feet above the ground, and which was to all appearance horizontal. *Peal* describes the performance in steady breezes of 5 to 10 miles an hour, when small tufts of cotton from the *Bombyx malabaricum* are shown by the telescope to float beautifully horizontal at elevations from 200 to 2,000 feet, and *Basté* says, as indeed all observers will agree, that the manœuvre most frequently employed by the birds is that of spiral soaring, that it takes place in light steady breezes, and that it is represented in plan by figure 5. The bird starting from the point A descends with the wind to about the point B, whence, facing the wind, he rises to the point C, which is higher than A, and thence repeats the evolution, his circlings overlapping each other and the bird meanwhile drifting slightly down the wind. The dotted lines on the diagram indicate the descents, and the full lines the ascents, as figured by *Basté*. He also states that occasionally, instead of drifting

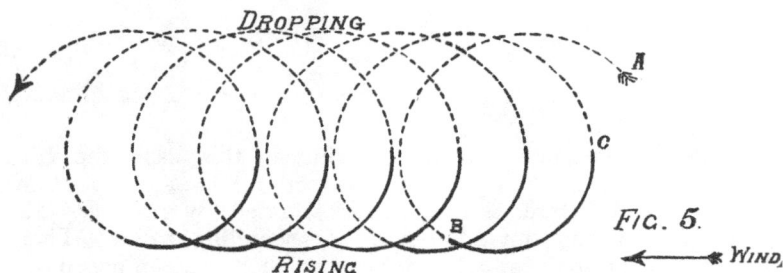

FIG. 5.

with the wind, the bird performs a manœuvre which brings him back to the original point A, describing in that case a closed ellipse instead of a circle, and that this is done by descending down the wind and by reascending on an undulatory course when coming back against the wind.

Now, this spiral soaring, performed on rigid wings in steady breezes of 5 to 10 miles per hour which are apparently horizontal, and through which the bird maintains an average speed of about 20 miles an hour, is the mystery to be explained. It is not accounted for, quantitatively, by any of the theories which have been advanced, and it is the one which has led some observers to claim that it was done through "aspiration," *i.e.*, that a bird acted upon by a current actually drew forward into that current against its direction of motion.

Aspiration really exists under some circumstances. I have seen, hundreds of times, buzzards advancing against winds of 10 to 15 miles an hour, without losing altitude, for distances which precluded the idea that this was done at the expense of previously acquired momentum. On several such occasions I liberated bits of down which went off quite horizontally, but I am not prepared to admit that the wind was also horizontal at the bird. There are, to be sure, some curious phenomena which have been termed " aspirating currents." *Dr. Thomas Young*, the great physicist, showed in 1800 that a curved S-like surface suspended horizontally by a thread advanced against an air jet impinging upon its upper surface. *Professor Willis*, of Cambridge, demonstrated that a light disk, placed parallel to and very close to another disk in which a tube was inserted, rose up against the blast when air was blown through the tube, and we now have the modern " ball nozzle," in which a ball is aspirated to and held suspended in a conical adjutage through which a stream of water or of air is issuing; but in every such case we can show that the force exerted is greater than the reaction produced through rarefaction, and these phenomena do not help us to explain the possibility of " aspiration " for a bird immersed in a current.

The simplest and most satisfactory explanation is to admit that there is an ascending trend of wind at the bird, and then propulsion can be accounted for, as has been done for the gull patrolling along the steamer; but even this could not be figured out without the Lilienthal coefficients based upon experiments with arched surfaces. An inspection of these will show that between angles of $+ 6°$ and $0°$ the lift is from 3 to 12 times what it would be with planes of equal area, while at angles between $+ 3°$ and $+ 32°$ the tangential pressure, producing only friction on a plane, becomes a propelling factor, and thus, if the angle of incidence with the course be, say, $+ 3°$ and the angle with the wind be, say, $+ 9°$, sufficient reactions can be computed under a bird to support his weight and to propel him against the current.

I have inferred that these coefficients result from the peculiar shapes of sailing wings which have been shown in figure 1, in connection, probably, with the rolling or oscillating action which I have noticed in the wind; that the current passing over the upper surface produces a certain rarefaction which increases the pressure upon the lower surface by a certain amount due to an unbalanced pressure of the atmosphere,[1] while a part of the aerial waves encountered is reflected back under the lower sur-

[1] As the weight of the atmosphere presses in all directions 2,160 pounds per square foot, a rarefaction of $\frac{1}{1000}$ would result in an unbalanced pressure of 2 pounds per square foot.

face, just as a sea-wave is reflected by a wall and would tend to drag it forward if its top were suitably shaped.   That this action does not occur, or occurs in lesser degree, with other forms of wings seems to be established by the fact that the flapping birds do not sail, but only glide.

This is advanced simply as conjecture because I have made no instrumental measurements, but it may possibly serve to explain hereafter how the bird obtains energy from the wind.  I now believe that this action could not take place if the wind consisted of uniform horizontal films or layers, such as we generally conceive.   There is an analogous case for water.   A vessel adrift upon a smoothly flowing current cannot by any method be made to extract energy therefrom, but the same vessel adrift upon sea-waves can be made to propel itself against the wind and waves by a plane attached some distance ahead below the keel, which plane shall act on the water in the trough of the sea where the particles are oscillating towards the wind, and so drag the vessel forward.   It is conceivable that by a descent through waving horizontal wind, enough energy and speed should be gathered to rise in a light breeze higher than the initial point, but this is, as yet, speculative.

Direct aspiration against a horizontal wind cannot be figured by the Lilienthal coefficients.   It is my opinion that this is an exceptional performance, which requires an ascending trend, and that, besides, the wind must be stronger than for spiral sailing.   Aspiration therefore leaves unexplained the mystery of spiral sailing flight in light breezes if the latter be really horizontal.

The mystery vanishes if we suppose the wind to have a sufficient ascending trend; but the objection has been advanced that we cannot assume ascending trends to occur all over the sky (especially in cloudy weather), and that in point of fact spiral sailing is observed to occur promiscuously and continuously all over the sky.   *Mr. Maxim* presents the most reasonable hypothesis to account for this, *i.e.*, that there are ascending and descending columns of air, and that the birds seek out the former; but this hypothesis requires evidence that the sailing birds invariably keep over such ascending columns in their wandering spirals; that a thousand buzzards, patrolling a township by circling, find columns enough to support them; or that the frigate bird, going out one hundred miles to sea and back again in a day, performs his journeyings by the aid of ascending columns.

I am not prepared to advance any other theory of spiral sailing in light breezes. My own observations of the rotary action in wind currents are confined to a short distance above the surface, and *Mr. Maxim* gives good reasons for doubting whether this action extends to any great height in the air. It is worth investigating, but until this is done it would be speculative to base a new theory upon anything but ascertained facts.

Upon the whole, sailing flight cannot yet be said to be accounted for in all its phases. Its full explanation requires that it shall be shown how the bird extracts energy from the wind, that the conditions assumed actually exist at the time of the particular evolution considered, and that the manœuvres of the bird will produce the observed result. This must be supported by quantitative calculations based upon actual observations of the speeds of the wind and of the bird, the angles of incidence with their coefficients, and the distances traversed horizontally and vertically, so that a good deal more is required than has yet been presented, in order to carry conviction.

It may be added that the simplest and most satisfactory explanation thus far is that which assumes ascending columns or trends of wind to exist at opportune times and places, but that it does not account for the cases in which all observers are agreed that the wind is horizontal.

# THE WAY OF AN EAGLE IN THE AIR.

By E. C. HUFFAKER.

I HAVE seen the bird soar many times when, close at hand, there was no evidence whatever of any movement in the air.

But the senses cannot readily detect a warm current of air having a velocity of much less than four feet per second, and an ascending current having such a velocity would amply suffice to sustain the bird.

Of aerial currents he can only avail himself of those to which he can offer some sort of resistance, and the power which he extracts from the air is directly proportional to the resistance which he offers to its movements. From ascending currents he is able to extract energy through the resistance of his own weight, which, being a constant quantity and incapable of destruction by the winds, may be used continuously as long as the bird remains in the ascending current.

He may also oppose the winds with the inertia of his body. But this inertia, unlike gravity, cannot be indefinitely opposed to the resistance of winds moving in a fixed direction; so that it becomes an available source of power only when their direction is variable. But this variability in direction must be understood to include variations in velocity, since with regard to the mean velocity the variations may be regarded as opposite in direction.

Two classes of theories may therefore be advanced to account for soaring flight: the one based upon the inertia of the body, the other upon its weight.

The simplest theory is that the bird soars by means of ascending currents. But it is difficult to account for the existence of such currents under many of the circumstances of actual flight.

The vultures soar as often as they find a dead body, and will continue to do so for days, not only in the vicinity, but over the immediate locality in which the body is found, at least whenever even a light wind is blowing. Nor does the character of the surrounding region of country seemingly affect their ability to soar. And as ascending currents cannot exist at all times and in all places, but are more often absent than present in any given locality, it is difficult to understand why they should at all times be found in the neighborhood of a dead body.

This difficulty, however, will disappear if we suppose that the soaring bird is capable of producing ascending currents.

The immediate effect of the action of the wings upon the air is to drive it downward, as Maxim found to be the case with his whirling table. But under certain conditions of the atmosphere it is theoretically possible for these descending currents to give rise to ascending currents, which may increase in volume until the bird himself is carried up by them.

This may occur whenever the lower strata of air become superheated, or whenever the temperature in ascending decreases more rapidly than 1° F. for each 183 feet of ascent. Under such circumstances, if a bird begins soaring in circles, say 100 feet above the earth, the masses of air sent downward by his wings will continue to descend until they reach the surface.

Other masses of warm air must rise to take their place, and in this way channels are made through which an interchange is effected between the warm air below and the cold air above. This circulation once set up will speedily involve masses of air vastly greater than those first set in motion by the bird. The bird, as it were, taps the great reservoirs of energy stored in the lower strata of the air by the rays of the sun on every warm day. And it is noticeable that it is on warm days when there is little wind that the bird soars best.

Certain facts, not otherwise easily explained, give color to the theory. The bird usually soars for some time, often for several minutes, before he begins rising, where the ground beneath is manifestly destitute of prey. A current already in existence would carry him upward as soon as he entered it.

Hawks and vultures soar in companies when rising in circles and separate as soon as they reach a desired altitude. Acting in concert they could generate a rising current more speedily than when acting singly. Two will often be seen rising together to great heights, following each other on the opposite sides of a circle. I once saw two large hawks, at which I was trying to get a shot, rise from a dead tree in a wide river bottom, and after some vigorous flapping begin ascending almost perpendicularly in circles, until they were entirely lost to view in the blue sky above. The day was calm, and if a current rising to so great a height already existed near the spot from which they were frightened, it seems singular that they should have so readily found it. But if the heated air over the plain was in a condition to rise, great masses might have found an upward outlet through an opening made in the overlying strata by the hawks, and this opening the birds could as easily have effected at any other spot upon the plain.

But even if this theory could be shown to be correct, it would by no means offer a full solution of the problem of soaring flight.

It would not account for those flights in which the bird maintains his altitude without turning upon his course, as he so often does when the winds are high. This feat, which is known as "aspiration," is, I think, seldom or never accomplished except in strong winds; nor — except in the vicinity of wind breaks — is the bird's rise very rapid for long distances. In Mississippi I have seen scores of black vultures at various altitudes so soaring in a strong steady wind from the Gulf of Mexico over an almost level country. In the nature of the case these birds would encounter as many descending as ascending currents, and if they derived support from such currents, it must have been because the ascending currents were more effective than the descending, which is not an improbable supposition when we consider the construction of the bird's wing, with elastic quills and concave lower and convex upper surfaces. In the anemometer the instrument is kept in motion through the greater pressure upon the concave surfaces of the cups. The same principle applies, perhaps even more effectively, to wings. Besides, we know that by beating the wings in a still air the bird is supported and borne forward, and if we suppose the wings stationary and the air beating alternately upon their upper and lower surfaces, the result should be the same, provided, of course, that the wind beats were repeated with sufficient rapidity.

Professor Langley has shown that a horizontal plane, free to fall, descends far more slowly when driven edgewise through the air than when allowed to drop vertically. The same is true of a fleece of cotton exposed to a horizontal wind. On releasing two pieces of cotton from the hand, in what appeared to be a strong horizontal wind, I found that they were carried more than 300 yards before coming to the earth; others fell within 50 feet; still others rose until lost to view; others released in companies soon drifted widely apart. These bits of cotton must have soon acquired a velocity equal to the general velocity of the wind; yet in some way they were kept from falling as they would have done in still air.

If we suppose that the direction of aerial currents is continually changing, and that these changes at a given point occur at intervals of two or three seconds, "aspiration" may be accounted for.

Air ascending and descending in large masses might also be made available, since by descending through the falling and ascending through the rising masses, the bird would remain a longer time in the latter than in the former, even in direct flight.

The variations in the velocity of the winds can be made available by a bird having in general the mean velocity of the wind, by the resistance due to inertia, which may be alternately overcome in opposite directions. But it is not altogether clear how a steady advance into the winds may thus be made. No theory yet advanced, however, has found general acceptance, and a certain degree of mystery still surrounds the majestic flight of the great soaring birds.

In some way they accomplish the feat of remaining in the air for hours without flapping, maintaining their elevation, taking long journeys, rising, falling, moving with the wind or against it, gathering strength from the storm, and all with a grace and sublimity of movement unapproachable.

What may be termed the mechanism of flight is also little understood. We are ignorant of the form of the wing in flight, of its movements, and of the function of its several parts, as well as of the manner in which it penetrates the air and maintains its equilibrium through all the vicissitudes of flight.

The wing from which we take our measurements is not the wing with which the bird soars, either in general form, curvature, or detail of construction.

Our studies must usually be carried on from a distance, and when on rare occasions the vulture hovers for a few seconds overhead, with his great hollow wings outstretched to the wind, we are in danger of learning nothing, through our eagerness to learn everything. It is only when we come to search for the details of construction that we are able to make progress.

In this way, however, we may arrive at certain definite conclusions: that the fundamental form of the wing is a concavo-convex surface, with rigid front margin bevelled above to a

sharp edge, and set in the rear and at the outer ends with a row
of elastic quills, curved in all directions, each overlapping the
next outer quill, and together under pressure forming a firm
elastic surface; that the locus of greatest curvature lies near
the front margin, and that the elasticity is greatest along the
rear and outer margins; that the primaries are stronger and
more firmly set than the secondary and tertiary quills.

As a rule the wings of the soaring birds are not placed at
right angles to the body, but point forward, the front line often
forming a cupid's bow, as in the hawks.  Considering only the
broad expanse of the wing and neglecting the small front portion which slopes in an opposite direction, the angle of elevation of the wing is greatest across the primaries.

The wing, therefore, taken as a whole presents upon its under
surface a channel extending from tip to body, and so formed as
to deflect the currents inward and backward.  These currents
which cannot pass the stiff outer quills find an exit among the
more flexible secondaries.  In this way a pressure is produced
upon the forward portion of the under surface.  At the same
time the air above the wing tends to cross the wing, somewhat
at right angles, and to be drawn in by expansion from above.
This crossing of the upper and lower current produces a pressure much greater than would result if they moved parallel
across the wing.

The lifting power of planes, as determined by experiments
with whirling tables, is known to be far less than that of the
bird's wing.  This may be due to the crossing of the upper and
lower currents described above, resulting in a slight degree of
compression and expansion.  Usually the wind passes an obstacle in its path as the water does with little change in density,
the resulting pressure upon the obstacle being due to the inertia of the displaced masses of air.  It is not to be supposed
that a plane with front edge elevated simply presses down the
air underneath.

If we allow that the air is thus pressed downward one inch
by a plane having a width of one foot, and that the disturbance
extends to a distance of ten inches below the plane, and that a
corresponding rarefaction takes place upon the upper surface,
then the resulting lift along the rear margin would amount to
the enormous pressure of more than 400 pounds to the square
foot, whereas we are fortunate if we secure a pressure of 1
pound per square foot.  In order to secure such a pressure it
is only necessary to alter the volume of the air involved by

$\frac{1}{4000}$ part of its original volume.   This results from the fact that the normal pressure of the air, both above and below the plane, is over 2,000 pounds to the square foot, and a change of volume amounting to only $\frac{1}{4000}$ would give a change of pressure both above and below of one-half pound, by a well-known law of the pressure of gases.

If we could readily compress the air in a free atmosphere artificial flight would be easily accomplished.  This is prevented in part by the rapid transmission of pressure, amounting in a direct line to perhaps more than 1,000 feet per second, and in part to the formation of compensating currents, by which the rarefied areas are relieved by a flow of air from the compressed areas.

Every one has noticed how loose windows rattle when a door is opened or closed.  If the door of a large church be suddenly opened the effect may be detected at the remotest part of the building, if a sash is loosened and all other openings closed.  So far as the ear can detect, this transmission of pressure is instantaneous, and it must have extended to every nook and corner of the building.  If, however, the door be held ajar and swung violently back and forth, no sound from the window will be heard, as the air has now formed a circuit for the transmission of pressure from one side of the door to the other.  A small opening in one window will also prevent the others from rattling when the door is opened or closed, the pressure finding relief in the outer air.

It will also be found that if the windows be closed and the door but slightly ajar, a perceptible pressure is required to close it quickly, and the windows will rattle again.  Here the air cannot complete the circuit from one side of the door to the other, and we have a rarefaction.

It seems possible that the deflection of currents in passing the wing may also result in compression and rarefaction, with a consequent increased pressure.

The form of the wing when pointed forwards adds to the stability of the flight, acting somewhat upon the principle of the Pénaud tail.  For the angle of elevation being least upon the following portions of the wing, those portions will be subject to greater changes of pressure than the leading portions, and so tend to maintain an even course of flight.  But a more important purpose is served in offering a path to the winds across the surface.

The imprisoned air within the concave surface must escape

along the lines of least resistance, and these are found along the rear margin of the secondary quills.

The result is therefore a uniformity of pressure upon the two wings and their several parts, which could not be obtained with a plane wing or one of cylindrical section.

The wings may lie in a horizontal plane, be elevated above it or depressed below it.   Usually the tips are upturned, but the rule is not invariable.

Birds which usually fly by flapping, as the crow and dove, sail with the wings depressed.

The centre of gravity seems to lie very near the centre of magnitude of the wing surfaces in ordinary flight, and slightly below the root of the wing and the plane of the tail.  The latter serves as a supporting organ in some of the soaring birds, and in perhaps all of the flapping birds.

In order to investigate experimentally the principles of soaring flight and the laws of equilibrium, I have constructed a number of artificial birds, or gliding models, which, on being released from the top of a hill or other elevation glide forward under the influence of gravity in a manner similar to that of the living birds.

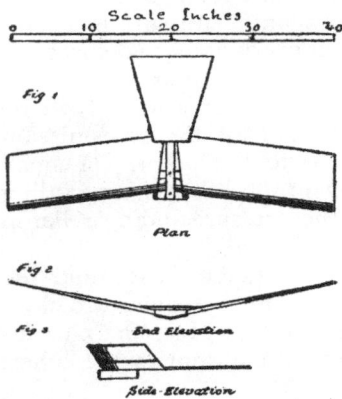

Figures 1, 2, and 3 show the form of one of these models.  It consists essentially of a body to which are rigidly attached a pair of wings and a tail.  The body and central tail-piece are made of oak, the frame of the wings and tail of some wood which is light, fine-grained, elastic, not easily broken or split.  The arm of the wing placed in front is bevelled above and hollowed out beneath like the wing of the bird.  The rear margin, unlike that of the nat- ural wing, is rigid, while the front and rear strips are joined by three ribs.  I have made the rear margin rigid because of the simplicity of construction which it allows.  The rear piece, however, is loosely attached to the ribs.

A cord does not answer the purpose so well as a strip of wood, since the yielding of the cord alters the entire surface of the wing, at the same time that it puts the main arm under a

strain to which it must, to a certain extent, yield.   Both wings
and tail are covered by stretching cambric over the upper surfaces, fastening it in place with mucilage.   The model has a
wing-area of two square feet, including the body, and when
complete weighs about eleven ounces.   Eleven ounces of lead
are added in the form of plates nailed to the body.   The model,
therefore, carries eleven ounces to the square foot of wing-
surface.

The main arm of the wing tapers from one-half inch at the
base to one-eighth at the tip.

As to whether this makes a flight of 20 feet or 2,000
feet depends largely upon relative adjustment of its several
parts.   The angle of elevation of the chord of the wing, regulated by means of wedges of wood driven between the ribs and
the main arm, should be greatest at the tips and least near the
body.   The tail should next be placed parallel to the middle
rib of the wing.   It should be fastened to the upper part of the
body by means of wire nails.   Finally the centre of gravity is
to be fixed by shifting the plates of lead.   It should be slightly
in front of the centre of figure of the wings.   The model should
be thrust lightly forward from the hand.   If upon trial it
mounts rapidly upward, the resultant of pressure passes in front
of the centre of gravity.   A new adjustment may now be made
in four ways: by moving the centre of gravity forward; by
decreasing the angle of the tips; by increasing the angle at the
base; or by altering the setting of the tail.   If, on the contrary,
the model plunges downward, the reverse of these alterations
may be made.   If the model flies well but descends too rapidly,
the angle of the middle or outer ribs should be increased.   If
the flight is undulating, the tail may be depressed or the centre
of gravity moved forward.

If the model turns to the right or left while maintaining a
horizontal position, the angles on one of the wings may be
altered.   If at the same time it descends rapidly in a curve
and comes down, no simple rule for rectifying the adjustment
can be given.   This is the most serious difficulty I have
encountered.

The fore-and-aft stability has given me but little trouble.
Out of thousands of experiments I have not made twenty in
which the model came down on its tail, and perhaps less than
one hundred in which it came down on its head.   Where the
model has either risen too rapidly or fallen too rapidly, I have
known what course to pursue to secure a better flight.

I have had no difficulty in getting rid of undulations. But where the model has come to the earth in a rapid curve, with one wing greatly raised, I have been for the most part utterly at a loss for a remedy. Nine-tenths of all my experiments have failed in this way, and I have known no principle which might be applied to overcome the tendency.

Elevated wings and tips, vertical rudders, keels, and lowered centre of gravity have been tried in vain. The difficulty lies in the fact that when the model moves in a curve, the outer elevated wing has a greater velocity, and therefore a greater lifting power than the depressed wing, which once being lowered shows no tendency to rise again. If with V-shaped wings, gravity tends to depress the elevated wing, the centrifugal force has the opposite tendency, and my experiments have demonstrated beyond any shadow of doubt that a model so equipped may and does come down in the manner indicated. My experiments, however, have led me on to a construction which seems to be free from this fatal tendency.

In any flying-machine it is of the utmost importance that no inert surface shall be suddenly called into action at the wrong time.

A concave surface in which the chord is parallel to the line of flight is usually a dangerous surface, for it may at any moment cease to lift at all, or it may suddenly have its lifting power doubled. Such a surface cannot safely be used upon the outer portions of the wing. Here the angle of elevation must be sufficiently great to insure constant pressures.

But such highly inclined surfaces cannot readily penetrate the air unless means of escape are provided for the imprisoned currents. This may be accomplished by giving a negative angle of elevation to the chords of the wing near the body. For the air rushing in from off the outer ends will insure pressure upon the inner portions as well. A twisted curved surface is therefore a safe surface. It has a greater lifting power than any other surface that I have tried, penetrates the air more readily, flies with a steadier movement, is less influenced by irregular winds, and, what is most important, it may be made to fly in curves with a slow rate of descent.

The philosophy of its action I have tried to explain in describing the flight of the bird. With such a model I have secured flights of 1,800 feet, with a fall not exceeding one in ten, when no wind was blowing. In a wind I have had it hover above a fixed spot with as much steadiness as that of the soaring birds.

I have also succeeded in so adjusting it that without a vertical rudder, and solely through the action of the air upon the wings, it would always turn into the wind.

It also gives a fair promise of soaring.

For the benefit of any who may be disposed to repeat these experiments, I subjoin working drawings showing the construction of the model in detail.

The construction is not difficult, but it is important that the work should be accurately done.

The body should be strong and the wings firmly attached by means of wire nails. The ribs should be fastened to the arm with springs and binding wire. It is not necessary that the cloth should be stretched very tightly, as a certain amount of curvature is desirable. The cloth may pass either under or over the end and rear pieces, which should be bevelled to fine edges. If desired, the inner portions of the rear margin may be made flexible by means of strips of cloth stiffened with mucilage.

But the disadvantages arising from the change of form resulting from the use of flexible margins are not offset by any marked advantage attending their use.

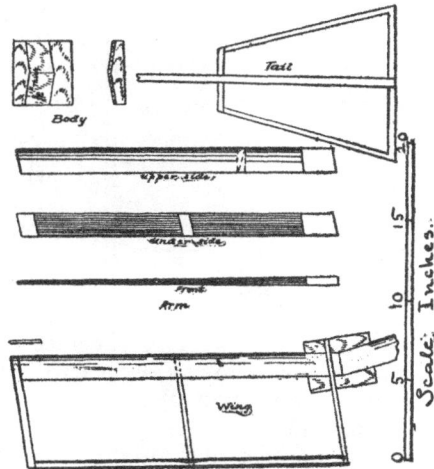

I have not found that the rigidity of the frame is objectionable. The elasticity of the air is more perfect than that of any frame that can be constructed, and if proper provision be made for its escape when compressed, its pressure will remain very nearly constant.

Besides, the elasticity obtained by means of an elastic cord along the rear margin is not the elasticity of the bird's wing, which pertains to the entire structure, including the arm.

An artificial wing, in which the torsion of the arm could be called into play, would be much more efficient than one with an elastic rear margin; for the pressure along the rear margin is but slight, and the yielding of a cord under increased pressure upon the entire surface would cause the wing to bag, and so make matters worse instead of better.

A concave surface properly constructed possesses great lifting power. In the bird the chord of any fore-and-aft section is but little inclined to the line of flight.

But its efficiency seems to depend upon the manner in which the currents pass it. They must follow the surface, as the formation of dead areas is fatal. Nature has provided the bird with a covering of soft feathers upon the under forward portion of the wing where the curvature is greatest, which by their elasticity insure a constant current across the surface of the wing. The accompanying figure shows some of the wing profiles which I use.

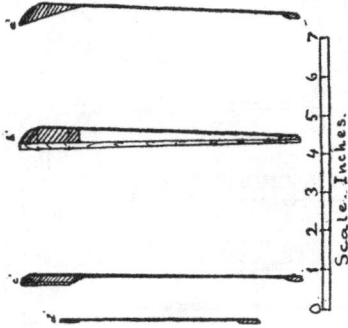

A current of air passing near a surface very nearly in line with it will be deflected by it, whereas it might break away from one greatly inclined to its course. This is true both of convex and concave surfaces.

A current of air blown through a pipe-stem against a lamp chimney will follow the surface through a quadrant.

Smoke so blown against a card will not rebound, but spread out in a plane over the surface. But a current passing an inclined knife-edge is liable to leave the rear surface altogether. The coverts referred to prevent this in the bird, for their elasticity keeps them pressed all the while against the current. The most effectual means I have found for preventing this in artificial wings consist in increasing the angle at the tips and compensating this by decreasing the angle near the body, for a steady movement can only be obtained when the general angle of elevation is small.

After a few changes the position of the centre of gravity may be left undisturbed and the subsequent adjustments applied to the wings and tail, more especially to the proper apportionment of the relative angle of elevation of the several parts. The angle at the tips must be sufficiently great to insure the requisite lift, and the reverse inclination near the body sufficient to accommodate the air from primary portions. It is chiefly upon this adjustment that the lateral stability depends. A vertical rudder may keep a model headed into a wind, but it offers no resistance to a tendency to turn upon a fore-and-aft axis, and it is in overcoming this tendency that I have found my chief difficulty. I have accordingly discarded the vertical rudder altogether, and depend wholly upon the setting of the wings for lateral stability.

When the angles are properly adjusted the model may turn through half a quadrant upon a vertical axis, while still maintaining its horizontal position.

All that is now necessary is to increase the resistance of the advancing wing. This may be done by increasing the angle of elevation at the tip. This should increase the lifting power of the wing as well, and so elevate it; but it appears that the resistance increases more rapidly than the lift. At any rate a wing is held back by increasing its outer angles.

I have met with a singular result in altering the angle of elevation of the tail. It often happens that depressing the tail causes the model to rise or descend more slowly than before. The explanation seems to be that while in this way the general angle of elevation is increased, the effect is most marked on the parts nearest the body, the centre of pressure being thereby lowered and moved backward.

A model properly balanced should maintain at all times a position approximately horizontal, under varying wind velocities. This is a matter of great importance and marks the difference between success and failure in a variable wind. If properly balanced a model may be carried upward to a great height by a strong wind upon a hillside, and will rise and fall without careening or plunging.

I have repeatedly secured such flights, and I do not doubt that it is possible to construct a model which would remain in the air an indefinitely long time.

The hill on which my experiments have been conducted has an elevation of about 175 feet above the valley at its base. About the summit and slopes of this hill vultures and hawks are daily to be seen soaring. Occasionally my models fly for a short time as well as the birds. On one occasion while standing on the summit in what appeared to be a dead calm, a model on being thrust lightly forward mounted upward several feet and sailed away horizontally.

In winds I have many times secured such flights, many of them being several hundred feet in extent. *The birds but do continually what my models do occasionally.* From this hill the birds make journeys to the neighboring hills, usually by a descent, often without it, and seldom by flapping.  Then they repeat the manœuvre of ascending in spirals, sail away to other points, and so continue for hours uninterruptedly.  It is not alone upon the hills and their slopes, however, that they soar. They may be seen near the earth, over meadows, and in sheltered curves, wherever chance carries them.  But their predilection is for the hills.

I once witnessed a large hawk ascending the slope of a hill with the utmost difficulty, being scarcely able by repeatedly flapping to keep clear of the earth.  On the summit the land spread out in a level platoon over which the wind was blowing, and into which the hawk mounted and advanced with all imaginable ease, not once flapping again.  Such flights as this are liable to mislead us.  We are ready to underrate the bird's powers of flight in the absence of winds.  In this instance the hawk not only flew up hill, but he did so in the face of a wind blowing down the hill.  It has not yet been demonstrated that the bird cannot maintain his altitude in a still air without flapping. Writers have been ready enough to explain soaring flight through the agency of ascending currents.  But it is equally certain that the bird would be borne down by descending currents, which are equally numerous, and with which he can contend only by flapping.  On the other hand it cannot be demonstrated by observation that the bird can soar in a calm. But we may safely assert that in fair weather with light breeezes, and in stormy weather with heavy winds, he may at all times soar.

It is not for lack of power that man fails to fly.  The winds supply it in lavish abundance, and if he is unable to make some sort of a flight with the power at his disposal, maintaining his elevation so long as the winds are favorable, he is not likely to fly by the use of engines.  The problem is one of equilibrium, not power.  Nor does flight require any delicate adjustment of the parts.  I have usually obtained my best results with models that were torn and battered by repeated falls. The birds, also, soar with broken quills.  I once witnessed the flight of a buzzard that had lost all the secondary quills from one wing and half from the other, yet his soaring was perfect, and he rose 500 feet without flapping.

When the bird wishes to soar in circles, one wing is depressed by increasing the weight upon it, while the tail is set approximately parallel to the elevated wing.  The angle of elevation of the latter is then diminished so that it penetrates the air more readily than the inner wing, and so travels with a greater velocity.

I have succeeded in adjusting a model so that it would fly in a curve and maintain a satisfactory rate of fall, but I have not been able to reproduce soaring flight proper, in which the bird, by moving in small circles, maintains his elevation in a wind.

Experiments with models in a wind blowing across a meadow seem to indicate that a horizontal wind has greater supporting power than still air, as the model will advance farther into the wind and advance more slowly than in a calm. I have not found that elevated wings offer any marked advantage over horizontal wings with upturned tips, and the adjustments are more difficult. Nor have I found any advantage in greatly lowering the centre of gravity. In the bird the wings are usually elevated, though there are exceptions to the rule. In one respect the bird has a great advantage over us, in being able to adjust his wings according to the varying circumstances of flight.

Models such as I have been using must encounter all kinds of winds with no change in their adjustments. However, a model which flies well in a calm will usually fly well in a wind of moderate velocity, often better.

In considering the results of these and similar experiments, it is well to bear in mind the relative importance of success and failure. A hundred failures through imperfect adjustment are offset by a single success. The successful experiment demonstrates the possibilities of an undertaking. I have thus been able to demonstrate that an artificial bird may glide through still air with a fall of three feet per second, so that a single-horse power would serve to maintain in horizontal flight a similar machine weighing 183 pounds; that it may be borne upward by light winds; that it may contend successfully with strong ones; that it may be made to automatically turn into a wind without the use of a rudder; that it may be made to come down safely; and that in almost every respect at least a distant approach may be made to the more perfect flight of the birds.

# SCREW–PROPELLERS WORKING IN AIR.

## By Hiram S. Maxim.

A GREAT English marine engineer in lecturing on the screw-propeller stated that recent experiments had shown that a piece of common boiler-plate riveted to the hub of a propeller was only five per cent. more wasteful in power than the most perfect screw that could be made, of course it being understood that in both cases the diameter and mean pitch were correct. I think, however, that if this same engineer had made his experiments with screws running in the air, he would have found a much greater difference.

The first screws that I experimented with were about 18 inches in diameter, and were attached to an apparatus in which the screw shaft could be moved in a longitudinal direction, its travel forward being opposed by a suitable spring, — in fact, this spring was part of the dynamometer that indicated the screw thrust. I remember on one occasion, while experimenting with screws, I found that, with a certain number of revolutions per minute, the screw thrust would suddenly mount on starting to, say, 21 pounds, and then fall back to 14 pounds. It occurred to me that this might be due to the momentum of the moving parts; that is, the weight of the moving parts, having been set in motion while there was little tension on the spring, might carry the screw shaft forward farther than was actually due to the thrust. I therefore limited the travel of the screw shaft in such a manner that it required 15 pounds thrust to move it forward. This of course would completely eliminate the factor of momentum. However, upon starting up the screw suddenly the dynamometer needle passed over to 21, the same as before, and then fell back to 15, the limit. These experiments went to prove that the screw, when started suddenly in still air, produced a thrust of 21 pounds, but when the current of air had become established, the screw would then be running in a rapidly moving current of air, and the thrust would only amount to 14 pounds, the speed in both cases being the same. Several other experiments were made which proved this to be true.

The screw-propellers employed in these experiments were made of light American pine, with a great degree of accuracy, coated with very hard glue, dried, varnished with shellac, and painted so as to keep their form.

At the beginning of the experiments, upon multiplying the thrust of the screw in pounds by the pitch of the screw in feet and by the number of turns that it made in a minute, I found that the foot-pounds represented were exactly like the readings of the dynamometer. At first I thought that some mistake had been made, because it appeared to me that the readings of the dynamometer ought to be more. However, upon attaching a pair of blades of the exact area and thickness of those of the screw, but without any pitch at all, I found that, notwithstanding the dynamometer was so sensitive that the touch of the finger tip to the shaft would move the needle, the power required for moving the blades in the air was not sufficient to be indicated. This demonstrated that there was no skin friction. Since that time I have found that a well-made screw is an excellent dynamometer for testing an engine. But all screws are not suitable for the purpose. A screw made exactly like those exhibited by the French government at the last International Exhibition in Paris, when tested in the same manner, showed that the useful effect of the screw in thrust was very much less than the readings of the dynamometer, while with any sort or kind of a screw that we were able to produce, consisting of a frame covered with a woven fabric, the useful energy in thrust never amounted to more than half the readings of the dynamometer, but when a perfectly made screw was employed, — that is, perfect on the face side, but very much rounded on the back in order to give great stiffness and rigidity, — it was found that the action was almost as good as with a thin screw. These experiments appeared to me to show that a well-made screw works very efficiently in the atmosphere.

I will mention another interesting point which will be useful to experimenters; namely, suppose that a small screw-propeller is making 2,000 turns a minute and, we will say, produces a thrust of 20 pounds without moving forward. Suppose that we now allow it to move forward, still maintaining the same number of revolutions per minute. Of course, as the velocity increases, the slip of the screw diminishes, but it is a curious fact that up to 50 or 60 miles an hour the actual thrust remains almost constant. What is lost in thrust by diminished slip in the air seems to be exactly compensated for by the advantages of running into new air the inertia of which has not been disturbed.

Another fact I would point out is that the thrust is greatly increased by a strong side wind, it being understood that the number of turns is kept constant. A side wind also had a great effect upon the flying machine on which I experimented. I often found that when the machine was running along the track at the rate of about 40 miles an hour, a side wind having a velocity of not more than 4 to 5 miles an hour would often produce a lifting effect of fully a ton on the upper rail, while the wheels on the opposite side would not be lifted off the track. The slightest movement of air across the track would always make the machine lift much more on one side than the other.

In regard to future experiments, I would say that the gun business has been very lively during the last year, that I have had much new experimental work to do, and that I have had very little time to devote to flying machines. I, however, have obtained very large premises with plenty of room, where I hope to resume experimental work as soon as I have the time.

---

## GLIDING EXPERIMENTS.

By Percy S. Pilcher.

*Experimental Department of Hiram S. Maxim.*

---

I MADE my first trials with a soaring machine in the summer of '95, having constructed the machine during the spring.

I had seen photographs of Lilienthal's apparatus, but I purposely made mine before going to see his so that I should not copy his details. I, however, went to see him fly before I commenced to experiment myself. My first machine had 150 square feet of surface and the wing tips were considerably raised above the body. At first I had a vertical rudder only, but I soon discovered that I could do absolutely nothing without a horizontal rudder. I found that it was quite impossible to control the pitching motions of the machine, and it was not until I had put on the horizontal rudder that I was able to leave the ground at all. This point is very clearly illustrated by experiments with model gliders. It is exceedingly difficult to make a glider with one surface only which will sail properly, but with two surfaces nothing is easier.

Although a machine in which the wing tips are considerably raised would always tend to right itself when falling, it is almost impossible to use such a machine for practising soaring out of doors, because although the machine is stable enough when the wind is right ahead, if the wind shifts and gets a little on the side it will press the weather wing up and depress the lee one so as to turn the machine over. But when I altered the shape of the wings so that they rose in the centre, but turned down again towards the tips, that is, so that the tips were scarcely higher than the middle of the machine, the machine became comparatively easy to handle, and I was able for a beginner to make some very good jumps. On one occasion when a man towed the machine by a string attached to the front of the machine I spent seventeen seconds in the air, and this is the longest time I have ever been off the ground.

During the summer I made a second machine which was straight transversely, although curved in the fore and aft direction. All the wing surface was considerably raised so that it was just above my head when I was in the machine, but with this machine I could not get along at all. When the weather became too cold I had to stop experimenting, and during the winter I built a new machine, which has 170 square feet of surface and weighs 50 pounds.

During the last summer I had to be very busy about other things, so that I have only had the machine out about ten times and have not been able to choose my days. In this machine I did away with the vertical rudder altogether. For days when there is not much wind the machine is quite manageable as it is, but for squally days I think that a vertical rudder should be added. With this machine I have twice cleared nearly 100 yards, once with a slight side wind and once in a dead calm. Most unfortunately I have never had the machine out when there has been a breeze blowing up the best hill for experimenting, or I should be able to give a much better account of its performances. Once when sailing fast I saw I was going to land in a big bush, so getting back a little in the machine I was able to rise a little and pass quite clear of the bush, although it was quite calm at the time; and I have also been able to steer sideways to a limited extent by moving the weight of my body towards the side to which I wanted the machine to turn. This is the first machine in which I have had any wheels, which are a great convenience for moving the machine about, and often save the framework from getting broken if one lands clumsily. The wheels are backed by stiff springs which can absorb a considerable blow.

A new machine is being built which will have an oil engine to drive a screw-propeller. With this machine, without the engine, I drop 50 feet in 10 seconds; that is at the rate of 300 feet per minute; taking my weight and the weight of the machine at 220 pounds the work lost per minute will be about 66,000 foot-pounds or 2-horse power. When I have been flown as a kite it seems that about 30 pounds pull will keep me floating at a speed of about 2,200 feet per minute, or 25 miles an hour. 30 × 2,200 = 66,000 foot-pounds = 2-horse power, which comes to just the same thing.

An engine is now being made which will, I hope, exert enough power to overcome the losses arising from friction and slip, and keep the new machine floating horizontally. Of course for the same wing-surface the machine will have to sail faster in order to keep afloat with the extra weight of the engine, and more power than the 2-horse power will therefore have to be used.

About 170 square feet seems to be the best area for a machine of this class for a man of average weight; if it is made larger the machine becomes heavier, and is much more difficult to handle because of its increased size and weight, and if it is smaller its sailing speed becomes unpleasantly great.

Last June I happened to be in Berlin again, and Herr Lilienthal very kindly allowed me to fly off his hill with one of his double surface machines. A light steady breeze was blowing, and after the practice I had had with my own I had no difficulty in handling his machine, but I was very much afraid that with the superposed wings high above the machine, as shown in Lilienthal's latest machine, they would prove very dangerous machines, especially in squally weather.

I hope with the new machine with the engine that I shall be able to obtain results worth reporting in your next ANNUAL, but " we shall see what we shall see."

# MISCELLANY.

*Principal Contents :* — *Carbonic Acid or Air ?* — *Professor Zahm's Experiments.* — *Blue Hill Aerial Explorations.* — *A Keel Kite.* — *A Rubber-propelled Model.* — *Methods of launching Aerial Machines.* — *The Albatross.* — *Plates XVII. and XVIII.* — *The Secret.* — *Blue Hill Measurements of the Velocity of Flying Ducks.*

## CARBONIC ACID OR AIR?

### By Prof. C. H. Peabody, Mass. Institute of Technology.

Now that liquid carbonic acid is a regular article of commerce it has been suggested that it may be a convenient medium for supplying power to flying models. A statement of some of the properties of this material and of some results of calculations concerning it, together with a comparison with compressed air, may be of interest. It should be remarked that the properties of the liquid, and of the gas or vapor near saturation, are not very well known, and further that the calculations depending on thermodynamic relations are subject to a considerable unknown error, especially near the critical temperature, which is about 85 degrees Fahrenheit.

One pound of liquid carbonic acid at freezing point occupies a volume of about 31.8 cubic inches. Its expansion with rise of temperature is very notable; thus, at 60 degrees Fahrenheit it occupies 50.1 cubic inches, and at 80 degrees Fahrenheit it occupies 90.8 cubic inches.

One pound of gaseous carbonic acid at freezing point and at atmospheric pressure occupies 14,000 cubic inches. At 60 degrees Fahrenheit the volume becomes 14,800 cubic inches.

The pressure of the saturated vapor, or of the liquid, is 520 pounds per square inch at freezing point; at 60 degrees Fahrenheit the pressure is 777 pounds, and at 80 degrees Fahrenheit it is 1,008 pounds, absolute.

The problem of interest for the experimenter is to determine the amount of energy that can be derived from one pound of the fluid. In dealing with this problem it must be considered that in the short time of flight of a model, little if any heat can be derived by the fluid from without, and consequently the vapor formed must be vaporized at the expense of the liquid remaining, which liquid will consequently be cooled to a low temperature. An approximate calculation shows that if we start with one pound of liquid at 60 degrees Fahrenheit, and continually withdraw dry saturated vapor till the temperature of the remaining liquid is reduced to 15 degrees Fahrenheit, about .28 of a pound of vapor will be formed and .72 of a pound of liquid will remain. The primary reason why I limited the calculation to this temperature is that the properties of the substance for lower temperatures are unknown; it may be admitted that 15 degrees Fahrenheit is a sufficiently low temperature for the experimenter, although the pressure of the fluid is then still very high, amounting to 243 pounds to the square inch.

Let it be assumed that the vapor as formed is drawn through a reducing value and is used at a pressure of 60 pounds above the atmosphere. Now, a perfect gas under such circumstances does not change its temperature appreciably when its pressure is reduced by passing it through a partially opened valve, but an imperfect gas does. What the change may be for carbonic acid cannot be readily determined from its known properties; there will not be a very large error if the change is neglected. The average temperature will be assumed to be $22\frac{1}{2}$ degrees, beginning at 60 degrees and falling as low as 15 degrees Fahrenheit.

One .28 of a pound of carbonic acid at $22\frac{1}{2}$ degrees Fahrenheit, and at 60 pounds above the atmosphere, will occupy about 756 cubic inches. Suppose that we decide to use it in a simple engine exhausting against the pressure of the atmosphere and with the valve set to cut off at three-fourths of the stroke. Assume further that this engine is to run two minutes and to make a thousand revolutions per minute. Such an engine will have a piston displacement of 0.2521 of a cubic inch, and may be given a stroke of one inch and a diameter of $\frac{9}{16}$ of an inch.

A calculation for the horse-power of the engine gives 0.073 horse-power, not allowing for defects or losses. It may be safe to assume that 0.06 of an indicated horse-power will be realized, and that 0.05 of a horse-power will be transmitted to the propeller.

Should the experimenter be content to fly the model one minute only, then the engine may be made twice as large and the power for the time chosen will be twice as great. Again, if he wants to run the engine at half the speed he may make it twice as large and get from it the same power.

Considerable more power may be obtained if the gas is used at a higher pressure and with more expansion. Suppose, for example, that the pressure is made 150 pounds above the atmosphere, and that a compound engine is used which has the large cylinder three times as large as the small cylinder; suppose that the cut-off is still kept at three-fourths of the stroke. In such case the piston displacement may be made 0.1143 of an inch, and the engine may have a stroke of $\frac{7}{8}$ of an inch, while the diameters of the cylinders will be $\frac{13}{32}$ of an inch and $\frac{23}{32}$ of an inch.

The calculated horse-power for such an engine is about 0.12; the indicated power may be assumed to be 0.085, and the power transmitted to the propeller 0.07.

At first sight it appears as though there will be an advantage in flying the model where the temperature is higher, as then the pressure of the fluid is higher and more will be vaporized before the lower limit of temperature is reached. There is also a gain of about two per cent. from using the fluid at a higher temperature at the engine. Unfortunately the entire gain is much more than offset by the fact that the reservoir will hold a less weight at a higher temperature.

Let us now make a comparison with compressed air, and assume that we must have the same volume at 60 pounds pressure at the engine in order to generate the same power, air being very nearly a perfect gas will experience little change of temperature in passing through the reducing valve from the reservoir to the engine. Let it be assumed that the air is used at 60 degrees Fahrenheit and at 60 pounds above the atmosphere. Under such conditions 756 cubic inches will weigh 0.17 of a pound, and this weight will occupy about 70 cubic inches at an absolute pressure of 800 pounds per square inch. Considering that some space must be allowed above the liquid in the carbonic acid reservoir for proper separation of liquid from the vapor, it appears that compressed air for developing a given power will occupy little, if any, more space, and will weigh only one-sixth as much. If, then, compressed air is readily obtainable, it will be found preferable for work on models.

---

## PROFESSOR ZAHM'S EXPERIMENTS.

PROFESSOR ZAHM, of the Catholic University of America, is determining experimentally the resistance of the air for speeds of one hundred feet a second and upwards,[1] by a newly devised method which promises unusual

---

[1] Man has travelled at the rate of 165 feet per second on the N.Y.C. R.R. See Aeronautical Annual, No. 1, p. 153.

accuracy of measurement. Bodies of various shapes, spheres, spheroids, cylinders, etc., are shot horizontally through a long room and caught in a barrel of cotton. During the body's flight its time of transit past three points in its path is recorded, and from this the velocity, retardation, and resistance are deduced. Thus in principle Professor Zahm's method is like the others known to the science of ballistics; but it differs from the others in three important details: (1) the measurements are made in still air at a uniform temperature; (2) the projectiles are made of wood which is from ten to twenty times as light as the projectiles commonly employed in gunnery, this making the resistance ten to twenty times more manifest, and hence the same number of times more precisely measurable; (3) the transits are recorded by the breaking of " screens " which have neither elasticity nor inertia.

The device for recording the transits is, perhaps, the most interesting feature of Professor Zahm's method. Three parallel streams of sunlight run squarely across the path of the projectile, and then are made to fall side by side on a photographic plate which moves at a known speed. Thus the uninterrupted streams trace three sharp parallel lines on the plate, and as the projectile crosses the streams in turn, short interruptions appear in the record whose consecutive distances apart serve to determine the time of the projectile's passage from stream to stream. With streams ten feet apart, for example, and a projectile moving five hundred feet a second, the duration of passage from one stream to the other would be one-fiftieth of a second. As the streams used are about one-hundredth of an inch thick, the time required merely to cut one so as to stop the light is, for such projectile velocity, one six-hundred-thousandth of a second; and it is found that, by use of the dividing engine, the records can be read with this degree of accuracy if, during the tracing of the record, the photographic plate moves at a speed of ten feet a second. By increasing the speed of the plate it would be possible to record the instant of the projectile's transit by a point accurately to a millionth of a second or less; but it is found that the above measurement of the duration of passage from stream to stream, together with the mass of the projectile and the distance between the streams, are all that is required to compute the resistance accurately to one per cent.

This research was begun at the Johns Hopkins University, and is still in progress in one of the private laboratories of the Catholic University of America. Professor Zahm hopes to publish in the next issue of THE ANNUAL the results of his investigations, and to express approximately the law of the resistance of the air within the proposed limits of speed.

---

## BLUE HILL AERIAL EXPLORATIONS.

### BY H. HELM CLAYTON.

ON August 4, 1894, a Richard thermograph, remodelled and lightened by Mr. S. P. Fergusson for the purpose, was lifted 1,440 feet above the ground with kites, by Mr. Wm. A. Eddy at Blue Hill.

This method of investigation seemed promising, and has been adopted by Mr. Rotch as a part of the work of the Blue Hill Meteorological Observatory, with the object of thoroughly exploring the air up to as great altitude as is possible. Active work was begun in July, 1895, since which date ascents have been made with considerable regularity and on an average twice a week, in all kinds of weather.

The first instrument used was a thermograph to which was soon added a barograph. In November a meteorograph was finished by Mr. Fergusson, which recorded temperature and wind velocity. This was used until May, 1896, when a meteorograph was received from Richard, of Paris, which records temperature, humidity, and altitudes by the barometer. This has, since then, been in regular use.

Cord was at first used for the kite-line, but this was replaced with great advantage by steel piano wire in January, 1896. At first, only 2,000 feet of wire were purchased, but a month later a mile more was added to the line. In July a second and in September a third mile was added. In the meantime, new reels had to be devised and strengthened to withstand the great crushing strain of the successive layers of wire, clamps devised for fastening successive kites to the line, a recording reel and dial made for indicating the amount of line run out at any time, instruments prepared to read the angles of the line and kites, screens invented and tested for protecting the bulb of the thermograph from heating by the sun's rays, formulas found for computing the height of the kites with corrections for the sag of the line, and other details worked out, all of which were necessary for accurate work.

A partial description of the apparatus is given by Mr. Fergusson in the " United States Weather Review " for September, 1896.

The development of instruments and methods required time and patience, but resulted in successively higher and higher flights, as seen in the following table :

| Date. | Altitude reached. | Date. | Altitude reached. |
|---|---|---|---|
| August 4, 1894 . . | 2,070 feet. | July 23, 1896 . . | 6,057 feet. |
| August 28, 1895 . | 2,536 " | August 1, 1896 . . | 7,333 " |
| January 26, 1896 . | 2,454 " | August 31, " . | 7,078 " |
| March 11, " . | 3,230 " | September 20, 1896 . | 7,356 " |
| April 13, " . | 4,593 " | October 8, " . | 9,375 " |
| July 20, " . | 6,591 " | February 10, 1897 . | 6,186 " |
| July 22, " . | 5,600 " | | |

These altitudes are above the level of the ocean, which is distant about six miles from Blue Hill. To find the altitudes above the point of starting on Blue Hill, subtract 630 feet from these figures.

The records obtained during most of the flights are clear and satisfactory, and promise to add many interesting facts to the existing knowledge of the atmosphere. We have found that, as a rule, changes of weather are encountered aloft before they are perceived at the ground. During cold waves the decrease of temperature as the instrument rises above the ground is found to be very rapid, until at a height of a mile or more the instrument may pass through the top of the cold wave, as happened on February 10. On January 19 the instrument was sent up in the midst of a cold wave, and at a height of 4,050 feet the temperature was found to be 16.5° Fahrenheit below zero, while at the same time at the ground it was 7.9° Fahrenheit above zero, showing the air to be more than 24 degrees colder at a height of 4,000 feet than at the ground.

Preceding warm waves the fall of temperature is usually very slow, and the air is sometimes much warmer aloft than at the ground, as on January 2, when, at a height of 2,800 feet, the air had a temperature of 56.1°, while at the same time at the ground its temperature was only 36.8°, showing a summerlike temperature above and a winter temperature below. But the most important fact which these kite ascents have shown is the sharp boundary between the overflowing warm currents and the colder currents beneath. The recording instrument reaches the top of the cold current and then passes very quickly into the warm current above, so that the temperature sometimes rises 20 to 30 degrees within a vertical distance of only a few hundred feet. This condition, which has hitherto received no adequate notice, is of very frequent occurrence, and plays a very important role in determining weather sequences. When the warm upper layer is damp its lower surface is chilled by contact with the lower current either through conduction or mixture, and a thick layer of cloud is formed which overhangs the earth like a blanket. When the warm upper current is dry no clouds are formed by contact with the colder current, but the warmer current acts like a wall beyond which the ascending currents caused by the heating of the air near the ground during the daytime cannot pass. In consequence no summer clouds, such as are ordinarily seen during the daytime of fair days, can form, and the sky remains clear throughout the day. If the warm current is found at the height of a mile, cumulus clouds may form, but the height of their tops is limited to the lower surface of the warm current and no thunder-showers can form. Ascending and descending currents are the chief factors in causing the gustiness of the air, so that in the warm current into which they do not penetrate the motion of the air is usually very steady. As a rule our records indicate a decrease of the gustiness of the air as the kites ascend, even when there is no change from warmer to colder currents, and at altitudes exceeding a mile the motion of the air is probably always very steady.

Sudden changes in the directions of the currents at different altitudes are very common and sometimes very great. Sudden shifts from south to west, or from north to east, are frequent, and in a few cases the kites have come into currents exactly opposite to those at the ground. On November 18 the kites were sent up in a north-east current, and when the height of about 1,000 feet above the hill was reached they quickly shifted around in a sort of spiral, and came into a strong south-west current above, so that kites on the lower part of the line were pulling in one direction and kites on the upper part of the line in another. The velocity of the wind usually increases with height, and not uncommonly becomes too strong for the kites.

The humidity generally increases until the level of the clouds is reached, when suddenly, as the tops of the clouds are passed, the air becomes extremely dry.

The diurnal changes in weather at the height of a mile are very different from those at the earth's surface. In our greatest ascents the recording instruments have been at a height of a mile or more for several hours, embracing in one case a large part of the afternoon and evening. The records indicate that the large daily change in temperature which takes place at the earth's surface is not found at the height of a mile or more. At this height the air is approximately as warm at night as during the day, and the only changes are those due to the passage of warm and cold waves. The daily change in humidity is, however, very large, and exactly opposite to that found at the ground. The nights aloft are very dry during fair weather, and the days extremely damp.

Up to the present time all the work of the ascent, including the winding in of the kites, has been done by hand by Mr. S. P. Fergusson, Mr. Arthur Sweetland, and myself, occasionally assisted by Mr. Rotch or some friendly visitor. The winding was done with a windlass, and the wire was wound on a strong reel. At present the cranks of the windlass are replaced by wheels, and a two-horse power engine winds in the line. This is expected to make high flights much easier to attain

---

## A KEEL KITE.[1]

### By H. Helm Clayton.

Since the beginning of the experiments at Blue Hill, in lifting meteorological instruments into the air by means of kites, we have felt the need of kites which can fly through a large range of wind velocity. The Eddy and the Hargrave kites which we have tried, if made light enough for light winds, are wrecked or disabled by strong winds or gales. In 1894 I tried the device of an elastic cord in the lower part of the bridle of the Eddy kite to lessen the pressure on the kite in strong winds, but the sensitiveness of the kite to changes in position of the point of attachment of the line rendered the device useless because the kite became unstable when the cord in the bridle

[1] From a paper read before the Boston Scientific Society on Feb. 23, 1897.

stretched.   In 1895 I tried the device of having the extreme parts of the side-planes hinged and held by India-rubber bands so that they could fold back in high winds.   This acted fairly well, but because the kite lost angular altitude when the planes folded back the experiments were not considered entirely satisfactory.   Finally, in February, 1897, profiting by the experiments of Mr. Lamson and some suggestions in Mr. Chanute's book on " Progress in Flying Machines," I tried the device of introducing a keel in the ordinary diamond-shaped kite.   This gave stability without the use of a tail, and enabled the kite to fly through a larger range of wind velocity than any kite we have yet tried.   The experimental kite I have made is not sensitive to the position of attachment of the kite-line to the bridle, so that the point of attachment can be moved through a considerable range without destroying the equilibrium of the kite.   For high winds the point of attachment can be brought well forward, so that the kite presents a slight angle to the horizon and hence a diminished surface to the wind.   In consequence the kite can withstand strong gales without too great a strain on its parts.   The experimental kite was flown in a wind averaging 12 miles an hour, and also in a gale averaging 45 miles with gusts exceeding 50 miles (indicated velocity). The slight inclination of the plane of the kite gives a great vertical thrust in proportion to the drift by the wind, so that the kite continues to fly at a good angle in gales, notwithstanding the increased friction on the edges and surfaces of the kite in proportion to area presented to the wind.   By introducing a spring or elastic band in the lower part of the bridle, the points of attachment may be so adjusted that the kite will present the best angle for flight (20° to 30° from horizontal) for light winds.   When the wind increases the stretching of the spring will cause it to present a smaller and smaller angle to the wind, thus preventing the great increase of pressure found on the usual

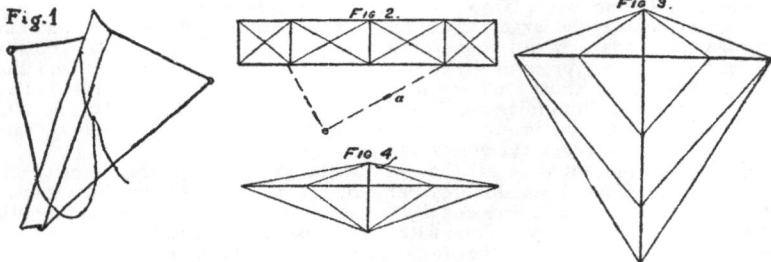

form of kites.   In this way it is possible to make the pull of the kite on the line much more nearly uniform through a large range of wind velocity than is possible with the usual forms of kites.   This is a very important point in sending up valuable instruments when safety demands that the strain on the line shall not exceed a certain limit which is somewhere between one-fourth and one-half of the breaking strain of the cord or wire, the factor of safety being higher with the wire than with the cord.

In brief, the points in its favor, many but not all of which are shared by the other kites which we have used, are: It is tailless; it is stable; it is comparatively simple in construction; it flies at a good angle and through a large range of wind velocity.   With a spring in the lower portion of the bridle it is partly automatic to changes of wind pressure, thus giving a more uniform pull than the ordinary kites.   However, the extent of this last advantage has not yet been fully determined.

A picture of the kite is shown in Fig. 1.

The method of construction is as follows :

A truss shown in Fig. 2, which corresponds with the vertical line in Fig. 3, is made for the keel out of some light and strong wood, as, for example, spruce. In my experimental kite this truss is 7 feet long and 15 inches deep. The sticks are ¾ × ⅝ inch, and there are four sections in the truss. The short sticks used for braces are fastened to the main sticks by strips of aluminium bent at right angles like angle-irons, and these are held in place by wrapping with twine. The truss is then guyed by a light wire (phospor-bronze was used in my kite). The wood is represented by heavy lines and the wires by light lines in the diagrams.

Next a stick of the same length as the truss, but somewhat stronger than any of the individual sticks used in the truss, is secured at its middle to the top of the truss at right angles to the frame and at about 20 to 25 per cent. of the length of the truss from the top, as represented in Fig. 3. In this figure the vertical heavy line in the centre represents the keel, which is seen edge on. The best position for the cross-stick has not been determined. When it is less than 10 per cent. of the distance from the top, the kite becomes less stable and more sensitive to the hanging, though it was found possible to fly the kite without any covering in front of the cross-stick. The covering (nainsook in my kite) is made large enough to fold over the keel and extend about an inch beyond the edges of the frame where it is folded over and pasted. It may be made to fit the keel smoothly by two strings passing from the front to the rear of the keel on either side outside of the covering and along the surface of the kite. Finally, two guys carried from the ends of the cross-stick to the lower ends of the keel, front and back, aid in holding the keel and cross-sticks in place. Though it is not necessary except for the strongest winds, a short stick may be erected above the keel and the cross-stick guyed as shown in Fig. 4. The places for tying the bridle are shown by the broken line under the keel truss in Fig. 2. The position of the spring is shown at *a*. It is necessary in this kite, as in others of this type, to take great care to have the centre of the cross-stick over the keel and the cross-stick as nearly at right angles to the keel as possible, so that there shall be the same amount of surface on each side of the keel below the cross-stick. Otherwise the kite will fly to one side and not directly into the wind. If the cover over the rear end of the keel is drawn tight at the bottom so as to form a V the stability is increased, but this is usually not necessary.

---

## A RUBBER-PROPELLED MODEL.

COMPLYING with a request, Dr. Langley has kindly sent the following description of one of the early models referred to in his article:

*Model No. 26.* — This model was constructed anterior to May, 1891. Its motive power is twisted India-rubber, carried in tubes of paper stiffened by shellac, these tubes serving at the same time to form a part of the frame and give strength to the construction.

There are two pairs of wings, one over the other, spreading 83 cm. The upper wing is 14, and the lower 19 cm., from front to rear. The area of the upper is 1,148, and of the lower 1,634 cm. Each wing makes a large diedral angle (about 165 degrees) with the others. They are nearly flat, with a very slight curvature toward the tips, where they are strengthened in each case by three light, very thin strips of wood, which are only indicated in the drawing. The ribs of the wings are of hickory, and their surfaces of silk, strengthened with these thin pieces of wood toward the extremities. They are guyed with fine wires, and both pairs can be slid forward or back to obtain the requisite balance.

The area of the horizontal tail is 144 cm. This tail, it is important to notice, is carried on the end of a long and *elastic* rod, and is intended to be set at an angle with the plane of the wing as in the Pénaud original design.[1]

---

[1] The importance of the elastic feature in the Pénaud aeroplane tail is insisted on in the article on Flight in the 9th ed., Encyclo. Brit., quoted on pp. 164 and 165 of this number of THE ANNUAL.

There are two propellers.  These are made of a central rib of wood, with blades of paper stiffened with glue.  Their diameter is 23 cm., and width·of blade about 5 cm.  There are 100 turns of rubber within each paper tube, the

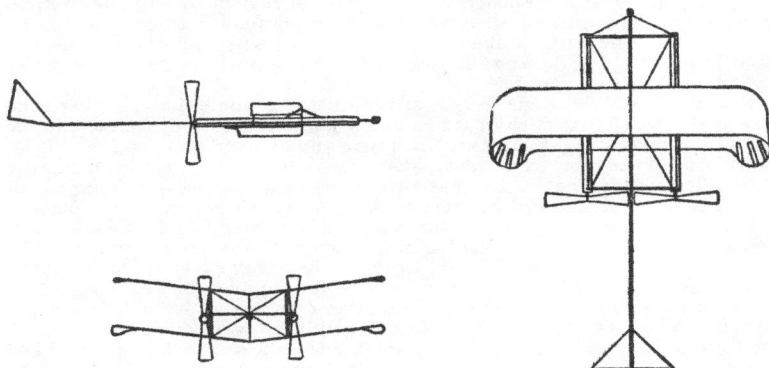

tension from which is applied directly to the propellers, each of which revolves on a journal· passing through a piece of cork, which can be withdrawn from the tube.

The total weight of No. 26, including frame, rubber, wings, and tail, is 156 grammes.  (In this model the area of the wings bears a much larger proportion to the weight than is usual, being at the rate of nearly 8 feet of surface to the pound of weight.)  There is no record of the length of flight attained by this model.  None of the flights of the other models exceeded 100 feet.

## METHODS OF LAUNCHING AERIAL MACHINES.

LARGE soaring birds commonly begin their flights by running toward the wind upon land or water, or by dropping from an elevated perch.  No aerial machine sustained by aerocurves is under the conditions requisite for free flight until, relatively to the wind, it has a certain velocity.  Dr. Langley has told [1] of the difficulties which he has encountered and overcome in launching his aerodrome.  In conversation recently, he suggested another method of

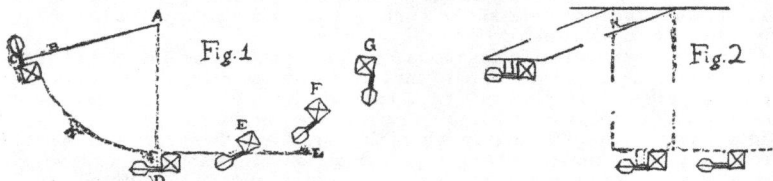

launching which will commend itself to experimenters with models.  This consists in using an apparatus which he calls the *double pendulum.*  The problem is to hold an aerodrome firmly in its place while velocity is being given to it, and to effect its release at just the instant when its velocity and direction are those requisite for satisfactory free flight.  Before the double pendulum is described the defects of the single pendulum must be indicated.

[1] See p. 21 *et seq.*

In Fig. 1, AB is a pendulum supported at A; C is an aerodrome clamped to a frame at the free end of the pendulum in such a manner that automatic release is given to it when it has just passed the position D. Now, if the backbone of the aerodrome is horizontal at D, the aerodrome, instead of going in the desired course toward L, takes an upward course DEFG, and soon it is pointed toward the zenith. The cause of this is as follows: the aerodrome, when clamped to the pendulum, partakes of the rotary motion of the latter round the point A, its upper side is toward A as the face of the moon is toward the earth, yet the release of the aerodrome in nowise deprives it of its rotary motion, and thus the positions seen at EFG are accounted for. Turning now to Fig. 2 we see how the double pendulum remedies the defect, and how, by its use, an aerodrome may be launched unhandicapped. One important merit of this double pendulum apparatus, as mentioned by Dr. Langley, is that it contains no elements which unfit it for use on a large scale for a man-carrying machine. Dr. Langley further suggests that the pendulum be made as light as is compatible with strength, and that a powerful spring be used to give it motion, this being much quicker in its action than the force of gravity.

-------

### THE ALBATROSS.

THE contour of the albatross, shown in Figure 2, Plate XVIII., is taken from Alfred Newton's " Dictionary of Birds," and the following quotation comes from the same source: "In process of time the name has become definitely limited to the larger species of *Diomedeidæ*, a family of the group *Tubinares*, and especially to the largest species of the genus *Diomedea exulans*, the 'Man-of-war bird' or wandering albatross of many authors. Of this, though it has been so long the observed of all observers among voyagers to the Southern Ocean, no one seems to have given, from the life, its finished portrait on the wing, and hardly such a description as would enable those who have not seen it to form an idea of its look.

"The diagrammatic sketch by Captain (now Professor) Hutton, here introduced, is probably a more correct representation of it than can be found in the conventional figures which abound in books. The ease with which this bird maintains itself in the air, 'sailing' for a long while without any perceptible motion of its wings, whether gliding over the billows, or boldly shooting aloft again to descend and possibly alight on the surface, has been dwelt upon often enough, as has its capacity to perform these feats equally in a seeming calm or in the face of a gale; but more than this is wanted, and one must hope that a series of instantaneous photographs may soon be obtained which will show the feathered aeronaut with becoming dignity.

"The most vivid description is perhaps that given by Mr. Froude in his ' Oceana,' of which a part may here be quoted. 'The albatross wheels in circles round and round, and forever round the ship, now far behind, now sweeping past in a long rapid curve, like a perfect skater on an untouched field of ice. There is no effort; watch as closely as you will, you rarely or never see a stroke of the mighty pinion. The flight is generally near the water, often close to it. You lose sight of the bird as he disappears in the hollow between the waves, and catch him again as he rises over the crest; but how he rises and whence comes the propelling force is to the eye inexplicable; he alters merely the angle at which the wings are inclined; usually they are parallel to the water and horizontal, but when he turns to ascend, or makes a change in his direction, the wings then point at an angle, one to the sky, the other to the water.'

"The mode in which the ' sailing' of the albatross is effected has been much discussed, but there can be little doubt that Professor Hutton is right in declaring ("Ibis," 1865, p. 296) that it is only ' by combining, according to the laws of mechanics, this pressure of the air against his wings with the force of gravity, and by using his head and tail as bow and stern rudders, that the albatross is enabled to sail in any direction he pleases, so long as his momentum lasts.'

" Much discrepancy, at present inexplicable, exists in the accounts given by various writers of the expanse of wing in this species. We may set aside as a gross exaggeration the assertion that examples have been obtained measuring 20 feet, but Dr. George Bennett, of Sydney, states that he has ' never seen the spread of the wings greater than 14 feet.' Recently Mr. J. F. Green says that, out of more than one hundred which he had caught and measured, the largest was 11 feet 4 inches from tip to tip, a statement exactly confirmed, he adds, by the forty years' experience of a ship-captain who had always made a point of measuring these birds, and had never found one over that length.

" In the adult bird the plumage of the body is white, more or less mottled above by fine wavy bars, and the quill feathers of the wings are brownish-black. The young are suffused with slaty brown, the tint becoming lighter as the bird grows older. It is found throughout the Southern Ocean, seldom occurring northward of latitude 30° S., and is invariably met with by ships that round the Cape of Good Hope or pass the Strait of Magellan."

The " London and Edinburgh Philosophical Magazine" (1869) contains a paper by Professor Hutton, in which the air resistances encountered by the albatross are mathematically discussed. Professor Hutton estimates the weight of an albatross at 16 pounds and the area of contour as 8 square feet. He dissents from the view expressed by the Duke of Argyll and Dr. Pettigrew, that the extremely long and narrow wings of the albatross are the best for flight, and says that the vulture and the condor sustain him in this opinion. Compare the contours of the vulture and the albatross in plate XVIII.

---

## PLATES XVII. AND XVIII.

ONE who intends to study the phenomena of soaring flight must first familiarize himself with the instrument by which the feat is accomplished. The qualities of the wing, which are evidently provisions in regard to flexing and flapping, are probably of less importance to us than those qualities which conduce to sustentation and steering.

The bird's wing, in its construction and action, is one of the most exquisite of nature's works.

Plates XVII. and XVIII. are introduced here, not because the illustrations are needed for any special article, but because students who discuss aeronautical problems are in constant need of such drawings as these to illustrate their points, and they will probably here find them convenient for reference.

Dr. Pettigrew in writing of the albatross wing shown in Fig. 5, Plate XVII., said that he had the original wing in his possession and that it measured over six feet in length.

The following is taken, with permission of the publishers, from Coues' " Key to North American Birds": — Fig. 6, Plate XVII., " shows the bones of the right wing of a duck, *Clangula islandica ;* A, shoulder, *omos ;* B, elbow, *ancon ;* C, wrist, *carpus ;* D, end of principal finger; E, end of hand proper, *metacarpus ;* AB, upper arm, *brachium ;* BC, forearm, *antibrachium ;* CD, whole hand or pinion, *manus;* composed of CE, hand proper or *metacarpus,* excepting $d^2$ ; ED, or $d^2, d^3, d^4$, fingers, digits, *digiti ;* AB, *humerus ;* rd, *radius ;* ul, *ulna ;* sc, outer carpal, *scapholunare* or *radiale ;* cu, inner carpal, *cuneiforme* or *ulnare,* these two composing wrist or *carpus ;* mc the compound hand-bone, or *metacarpus,* composed of three metacarpal bones, bearing as many digits — the outer digit seated upon a protuberance at the head of the metacarpal, the other two situated at the end of the bone; $d^2$ the outer or radial digit, commonly called the thumb or *pollex,* composed of two *phalanges ;* $d^3$, the middle digit, of two phalanges; $d^4$, the inner or ulnar digit, of one phalanx; $d^2$ is the seat of the feathers of the *bastard wing* or *alula ;* D to C (whole pinion), seat of

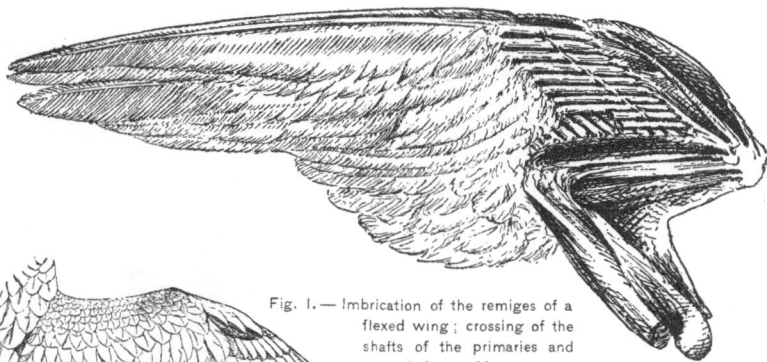

Fig. I. — Imbrication of the remiges of a flexed wing ; crossing of the shafts of the primaries and secondaries. — Marey.
— *" Le Vol des Oiseaux."*

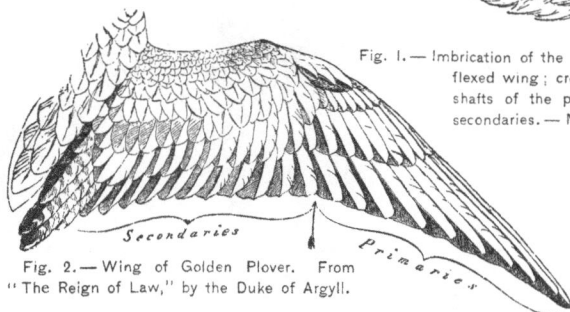

*Secondaries*
*Primaries*

Fig. 2. — Wing of Golden Plover. From " The Reign of Law," by the Duke of Argyll.

*Primaries*
*Secondaries*

Fig. 3. — Wing of Gannet. From " The Reign of Law," by the Duke of Argyll.

Fig. 4. — Right wing of the Kestrel. From Pettigrew.

Fig. 5. — Left wing of the Albatross. From Pettigrew.

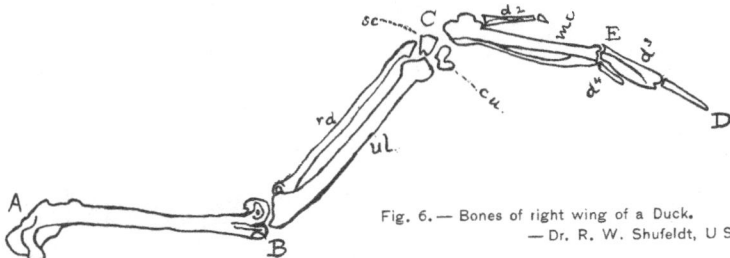

Fig. 6. — Bones of right wing of a Duck.
— Dr. R. W. Shufeldt, U.S.A.

Intentionally blank as was the original edition.

*Plate XVIII.*

Fig. 1. — The Bat.      From Pettigrew.

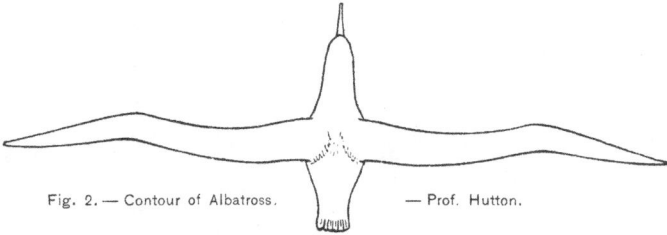

Fig. 2. — Contour of Albatross.      — Prof. Hutton.

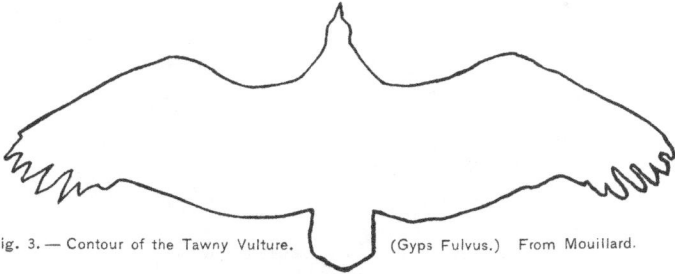

Fig. 3. — Contour of the Tawny Vulture.      (Gyps Fulvus.)   From Mouillard.

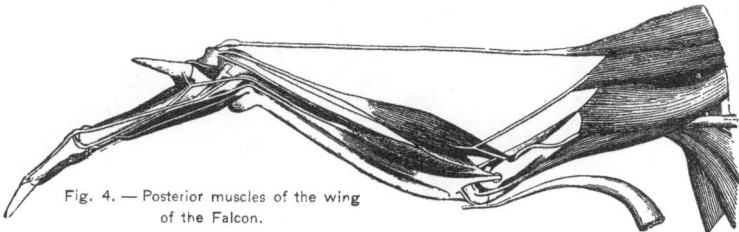

Fig. 4. — Posterior muscles of the wing of the Falcon.

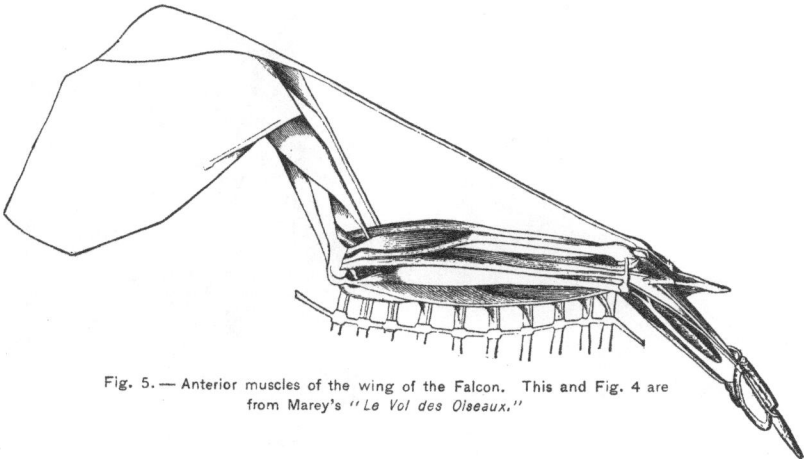

Fig. 5. — Anterior muscles of the wing of the Falcon. This and Fig. 4 are from Marey's *"Le Vol des Oiseaux."*

Intentionally blank as was the original edition.

the flight feathers called *primaries;* C to B (fore-arm), seat of the *secondaries;* at B and above it in direction of A, seat of *tertiaries* proper; below A, in direction of B, seat of scapularies (upon *pteryla humeralis*), often called *tertiaries.* The wing is shown partly spread; complete extension would bring ABCD into a right line; in complete folding C goes to A, and D to B; all these motions *nearly* in the plane of the paper. The elbow-joint and wrist are such perfect hinges that, in opening or closing the wing, C cannot sink below the paper, nor D fly up above the paper, as would otherwise be the effect of the pressure of the air upon the flight feathers. Observe also, *rd* and *ul* are two rods connecting B and C; the construction of their jointing at B and C, and with each other, is such that they can *slide lengthwise* a little upon each other. Now, when the point C, revolving about B, approaches A in the arc of a circle, *rd* pushes upon *sc*, while *ul* pulls back *cu;* the motion is transmitted to D, and makes this point approach B. Conversely, in opening the wing, *rd* pulls back *sc*, and *ul* pushes on *cu*, making D recede from B. In other words, the angle ABC cannot be increased or diminished without similarly increasing or diminishing the angle BCD; so that no part of the wing can be opened or shut without automatically opening or shutting the rest — an interesting mechanism by which muscular power is correlated and economized."

## THE SECRET.

ALBERT ROSS has the following in "Marine News" concerning " The Mystery of Soaring Flight : "

"If a bird can soar (*i.e.,* gain altitude without expending energy from within) in a uniformly moving horizontal wind, then he can also soar in a calm, for when he is in flight in the wind referred to, he is in a relative calm as soon as the resistance of the wind has overcome his inertia. There must be air *resistance* against his wings if he is to derive energy from the air, and when his inertia has been overcome (*if we understand the properties of air*) there can be no resistance against his wings, excepting that which is caused by the gravity of the bird, and gravity has never been found to give back to a body any more energy than that of which it deprives it.

"The question is, *Do we now understand the properties of air ?* Many careful observers have stated that they have seen gains of altitude made by soaring birds in cases where the influence of moving air seemed to be negligible. Some scientists reply, ' The observers were mistaken, the air currents were more potent than they thought.' That reply is distinctly unscientific.

" There is a use for the elastic rear part of the bird's wing which has not yet been discovered. It does not contradict the laws of thought to assume, for the purposes of experiment, that the constant action of the sunlight upon the air is such that when the air is agitated by the swift passage of the wing-bone, a molecular action is caused in the air which causes an expansion, and that the expansion, acting upon the rear feathers, upward bent, gives a forward thrust. The way to ascertain whether or not this theory is correct is to take air and churn it in a glass receiver under various conditions of light, temperature and humidity. I have suggested this to several physicists, and have been told that if the experiment were tried the results would probably be negative. Some physicists say that ' if there had been anything in this theory of expansion some one would probably have found it out before now.'"

## MEASUREMENTS OF THE VELOCITY OF FLYING DUCKS.

Contributed to "Science," of Jan. 1, 1897, by H. Helm Clayton : "Measurements of the heights and velocities of clouds are now being made at the Blue Hill Meteorological Observatory by Mr. Rotch as a part of an international scheme for such work. The measurements are made with specially constructed theodolites in which a large conical tube, with crossed wires at one end and an eyepiece at the other, replaces the ordinary telescope. "On the morning of December 8, while Mr. S. P. Fergusson and I were engaged in measuring clouds, a flock of ducks passed across our base-line, which is 2,590.3 metres (8,496 feet) in length. We succeeded in getting one simultaneous set of measurements on the apex of the flock, from which its height was calculated, and one or two independent subsequent observations, from which the velocity was calculated. The height was 958 feet above the lower station, which is situated in the valley of the Neponset river, above which the ducks were flying.

"The velocity of flight calculated from this measurement of height, and from the angular velocity measured at one end of the base-line, is 47.9 miles in an hour, and from the angular measurements made at the other end of the base-line is 47.7 miles an hour, making a mean of 47.8 miles. The wind was very light, having a velocity of only two miles an hour according to the automatic record made at Blue Hill Observatory, 615 feet above the valley station. The direction of the wind was from the north, and the ducks were flying from the north-east. These observations were not in our programme, but they may prove of interest to ornithologists and students of aeronautics."

---

A PRACTICAL illustration may perhaps make clearer the mutual action of the bird and the wind. The reader doubtless knows the "roller coasters" in which a car runs down one slope and ascends another, but never quite so high as the starting-point, because of friction and resistance of the air. Now let him fancy that, as the vehicle starts down a slope, the whole road-way moves in the contrary direction, gliding under the vehicle like the wind beneath the bird; his own mechanical instinct will at once indicate that the vehicle will then rise higher than the starting-point (if the route admits of this), the increased rise being produced by the action of the roadway gliding past. This may be verified by constructing a little apparatus, in which the roadway shall consist of an undulating, smooth groove, either straight or circular, and the vehicle shall be a steel ball, turned perfectly true and smooth. If the groove be straight in plan (undulating in side view), and mounted upon wheels, then two phases of bird ascension may be simulated:

1. The ball may be started down the slope, and at the same time the grooved roadway may be briskly moved in the contrary direction. The ball will be found to rise on the upward slope higher than the point it started from. This parallels the case of the bird which, already under way, breasts the blowing wind and rises on it.

2. Or we may place the ball at rest at the bottom of one of the curves, and by simply imparting quick motion to the roadway, the ball will be seen to ascend upon the opposing slope. This parallels the case of the bird rising above his perch by simply unfolding his plumage to the breeze. This, indeed, he may do without springing up; but in this case he generally drifts back a little, while, if he gains some initial velocity, he can rise and advance simultaneously, thus exhibiting a notable case of "aspiration."

To rise in circling flight lighter breezes suffice. This action may be simulated by making the groove circular in plan, and rotating the whole apparatus on a pivot. Its path may be made to conform to the bird's orbit by making a series of long, gentle descents, and of short and sharp ascents, the combination of the two occupying one round. Then, by rotating the pathway in one direction and starting the ball in the other, the latter will be found to ascend upon an irregular helical path; just as the bird drops a little when he is going with the wind and rises again, and higher up, when he sweeps against the current again. This last illustration is imperfect, inasmuch as the whole pathway has been made to revolve, while the wind utilized by the bird blows on as a current. It, moreover, takes no account of the irregular wind gusts which the bird utilizes. It also exhibits much more friction than the actual performance which we have tried to simulate.

What the bird does in a wind, man can do. Our muscular strength is much too small to progress by direct action like the flapping denizens of the air; but our brain is sufficient to supply simple guidance when we shall have acquired the necessary skill. So, if we add life to the aeroplane and a moderate muscular power to supply the guidance, to perform in the right way and at the right time those evolutions produced by birds in gliding flight, the author believes that man may succeed in riding on the wind. To compass this, to achieve simple journeying flight in elementary form, experiment, practice, acquired skill, are doubtless requisite; but of great daring or of fresh invention there is little, if any, need. The principles are known, the path is pointed out by observers of birds, and now success awaits the skilful, prudent man who will thoroughly understand what he has to perform. — *Mouillard, 1894.* (*Cosmopolitan.*)

FROM " L'Empire de l'Air," by Mouillard, 1881 (see Smithsonian Report, 1892) :

" The most stirring, exciting sight (the word is not too strong) is to stand in the vulture roost on the Mokatan ridge, near Cairo, and to look upon the *Gyps fulvus* (tawny vulture) passing within five yards in full flight. . . . All my life I shall remember the first flight of these birds which I saw, the great tawny vultures of Africa. I was so impressed that all day long I could think of nothing else; and indeed there was good cause, for it was a practical perfect demonstration of all my preconceived theories concerning the possibilities of artificial flight in a wind. Since then I have observed thousands of vultures. I have disturbed many of the vast flocks of these birds, and yet, even now, I cannot see one individual passing through the air without following him with my eyes until he disappears in the distant horizon. . . .

" The vulture's needs are few, and his strength is moderate. To earn his living he but needs to sight the dead animal from afar. And so, what does he know ? He knows how to rise, how to float aloft, to sweep the field with keen vision, to sail upon the wind without effort, till the carcass is seen, and then to descend slowly after careful reconnaissance and assurance that he may alight without danger, that he will not be surprised and compelled to precipitous and painful departure. And so he has evolved a peculiar mode of flight; he sails and spends no force, he never hurries, he uses the wind instead of his muscles, and the wing-flap occasionally seen is meant to limber up rather than to hasten through the air. And so the true model to study is the vulture — the great vulture. Beside him the stork is as a wren, the kite a mere butterfly, the falcon a pin-feather. Whoso has for five minutes had the fortune to see the Nubian vulture in full sail through the air, and has not perceived the possibility of his imitation by man, is — I will not say of dull understanding, but certainly inapt to analyze and to appreciate." [1]

As to sailing flight, none of the old-time falconers doubted in the least its existence. They observed it every day, and they knew that the wind was a necessary condition. Nobody troubled himself about an explanation in those days; but later on, when physicists attempted to explain the mechanics of flight and succeeded in conceiving the action of the wing stroke and the effects of air resistances, sailing flight appeared to them as a physical impos-

---

[1] Mouillard in his tables gives the following figures concerning the Nubian vulture : Weight of bird, 8152 grams; surface within contour, 1.11295 sq. meters; spread of wings, 2.66 meters; mean width of wing, .46 meters. One square meter sustains 7323 grams. Relative surface required to sustain 80 kilos., or 176.4 lbs. avoirdupois, 10.88 sq. meters, or 117 sq. feet, 16 sq. inches.

sibility.  They said that it was impossible to admit that a bird, suspended at a fixed point in the sky, should find in the action of the wind sufficient power to advance against that wind.    As well, said they, might we throw an inert mass into a flowing river, and expect the current to cause the body to advance up-stream.   And yet, modern observers have contested this verdict. M. d'Esterno and M. Mouillard demonstrated that, unless we absolutely disbelieve ocular evidence, we must accept the actual fact that sailing flight is possible, even if we have to admit that our present mechanical knowledge is insufficient to explain it. — *Marey.   Inst. of France.*

LILIENTHAL wrote as follows under date of April 17, 1896: "I am now engaged in constructing an apparatus in which the position of the wings can be changed during flight in such a way that the balancing is not effected by changing the position of the centre of gravity of the body.   In my opinion this means considerable progress, as it will increase the safety.   This will probably cause me to give up again the double sailing surfaces as it will do away with the necessity which led me to adopt them."

FLAPPING wings may be imitated, but only with small models ; the increased strength and weight of material necessary for larger apparatus, and the great motive power required for alternative action, have proved to be obstacles not yet overcome. — *Mouillard, 1894.*

WE   must not allow ourselves to be deceived as to the form of the bird's wing.   It is always more curved when not spread than when the bird is resting its weight upon it in the air.   Besides which, the curve, which in the beginning appears to be considerably stronger towards the front edge, becomes somewhat more uniform as soon as the quills are bent straighter at their roots by the pressure of the air from beneath.— *Lilienthal, March, 1895.*

MY investigations concerning the effects of curved wings had one result which was quite unexpected, namely, that the air resistance is not perpendicular to the chord of the profile curve, but that in certain impact angles of the air its direction inclines forward, with a perceptible drawing component.[1] — *Lilienthal, March, 1895.*

LILIENTHAL wrote, May 28, 1896: "I would finally remark that bodily strength and dexterity are of less consequence than the general intelligence and the gift of perception in technical matters when selecting the men [for gliding experiments]."

OBSERVATIONS OF THE FLIGHT OF BIRDS, by Leonardo da Vinci, Darwin, Sir George Cayley, the Duke of Argyll, Chanute, Lilienthal, Maxim, and others may be found in Nos. 1 and 2 of the Aeronautical Annual.

---

[1] *Mit nicht unerheblich ziehender Componente.*
  For Lilienthal's mathematical treatment of this subject see " Zeitschrift für Luftschiffahrt," February and March, 1895, and also the very interesting manual entitled "Taschenbuch für Flugtechniker und Luftschiffer," by Captain H. W. L. Moedebeck, published by W. H. Kühl, Berlin, 1895.

# EDITORIAL.

Please address Communications to
THE EDITOR OF THE AERONAUTICAL ANNUAL,
CARE OF W. B. CLARKE & CO.,
COR. PARK & TREMONT STS.,
BOSTON, MASS., U.S.A.
Cable address: JASMEANS, BOSTON.

*The publishers have remaining a few copies of the Annual No. 1 for 1895 and No. 2 for 1896. Price, postpaid, One Dollar each.*

## THE SCIENTIFIC VALUE OF FLYING MODELS.

THE ultimate object of aeronautical study and experiment is, of course, to hasten the time when it shall be possible to construct a *practical* flying machine.

There are some experimenters who think that the day of the great achievement will come sooner if in the immediate future we give the most of our time and thought to the development of the motorless air-sailer. Others think that more rapid progress will be made through the development of the self-propelled aerodrome.

It is quite needless to attempt at this time to say who is right; time will show us all that. Moreover, as stated in the introductory note, whichever branch of work is seriously undertaken by an individual, he may be sure that while working upon his own specialty he is helping those engaged in the others toward their common goal.

The supreme importance which attaches to the flying model comes from the fact that experiments with it may be made to lessen the number of risks of human life and limb. We have now reached the stage of experiment where it is necessary to use all possible persuasion to keep reasonably near *terra firma* those persons who have nothing but the courage of ignorance

(161)

to equip them for ventures in the air. A part of the glory of the work of '96 at Camp Chanute comes from the fact that no one of the experimenters was injured, all being under the control of an accomplished scientist, firm and clear-headed. If the lamented Lilienthal, with his great knowledge of engineering, his long experience, and his superb self-control, could come to his untimely end, is Fate likely to be kind to the novice?

Remembering that Lilienthal said, " It is not every man's business to launch himself into space," and knowing that there are some men who are so situated that experiments with models are the only ones which they can undertake, let us consider the possible value of the results of such experiments.

We can readily see that many models otherwise excellent will have limitations to their usefulness because of the laws governing the strength of materials. In designing a model it is advisable to keep in mind, so far as possible, the probability of the retention of its good qualities in case its enlarged counterpart is constructed. We know that the elements of strength contained in the model, which will also appear in a full-sized machine, are those which have come from the engineering skill shown in the structure, and that these elements must be so far in excess of the actual needs of the model that they will offset the great loss in the proportional strength of materials which occurs when the size of machines is increased.

I once knew of an imposing piece of experimental apparatus, having several hundred square feet of surface, which was withered by the wind because the designer had forgotten the simple point just mentioned.

It is not necessary to immediately settle the question as to how far the performance of a model is a *demonstration* of what can be done with its enlarged counterpart; it is enough for the present to know that experiments with models can throw much light upon several subjects that are now imperfectly understood. The following are some of these:

1. Automatic devices for preserving equilibrium.
2. Disposition of surfaces.
3. Placing of screws.

4. Curves of surfaces.
5. Relation of weight to area.
6. Relation of power to weight.
7. Effects of elasticity in sustaining surfaces.

Any one of these subjects is enough to occupy an experimenter for a long time.

In regard to the first subject it will be noticed that the contributors to THE ANNUAL have given no detailed descriptions of the automatic devices which they have tried. This is because of the conservatism which leads every rational experimenter to withhold details from the public until his own tests have satisfied him that the proper time has come to make an announcement.

Mr. Chanute in his book[1] describes many attempts which have been made to secure automatic equilibrium, and it goes without saying that no one will begin any kind of aeronautical experiment until he has given to that book the most thorough study. It may here be said that rolling balls, shifting mercury ballast, and pendulum devices to move rudders have been tried, but none of these have so far given satisfactory results.

If there is one man whose name is mentioned oftener than that of any other in connection with the subject of automatic equilibrium it is that of Alphonse Pénaud,[2] whose flying models attracted much attention twenty years ago and recently have attracted still more.

In 1874 Mr. T. J. Bennett, of Oxford, brought Pénaud's automatic rudder to the notice of the Aeronautical Society of Great Britain, in the following words:

But all the above models flew by accident, there being no special means provided for maintaining the equilibrium fore and aft. This problem M. Pénaud has solved by means of his automatic rudder. . . .

At last the idea occurred to him of placing a small horizontal rudder behind the sustaining planes, and inclined at a small angle to them. It succeeded perfectly. Its mode of action is as follows:

The centre of gravity of the machine is placed a little in front of the centre of pressure of the aeroplane, so that it tends to make the model descend an

---

[1] "Progress in Flying Machines." Published by M. N. Forney, N.Y., 1894.

[2] A Frenchman, now of honored memory, who died in sorrow and disappointment in 1880, before reaching the age of thirty years. See "Progress in Flying Machines," pp. 117-122.

incline; but in so doing it lessens the angle of inclination of the aeroplane, and the speed is increased. At the same time the angle of the horizontal rudder is increased, and the pressure of air on its upper surface causes it to descend; but as the machine tends to turn round its centre of gravity, the front part is raised and brought back to the horizontal position. If owing to the momentum gained during the descent the machine still tends upwards, the angle of the plane is increased and the speed decreased. The angle of the rudder from the horizontal being reduced, it no longer receives the pressure of the air on its superior surface, the weight in front reasserts its power, and the machine descends. Thus by the alternate action of the weight in front and the rudder behind the plane, the equilibrium is maintained. The machine during flight, owing to the above causes, describes a series of ascents and descents, after the manner of a sparrow.[1]

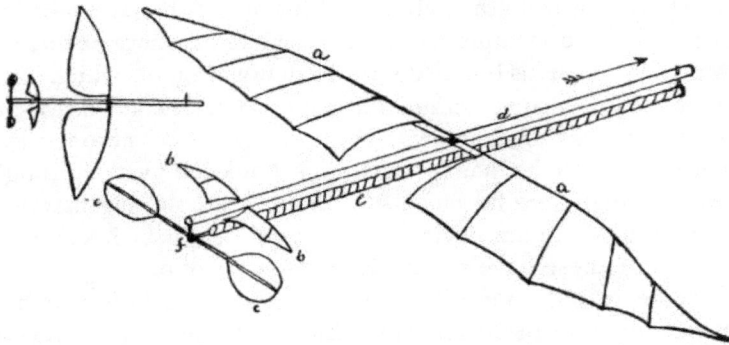

$aa$, elastic aeroplane; $bb$, automatic rudder; $cc$, aerial screw centred at $f$; $d$, frame supporting aeroplane, rudder, and screw; $e$, India-rubber in a state of torsion, attached to hook or crank at $f$. By holding the aeroplane ($aa$) and turning the screw ($cc$) the necessary power is obtained by torsion. — *M. Pénaud, 1872.*

There was one very important element contained in the Pénaud model shown in accompanying cut, and that was the *elasticity of the sustaining surfaces*, which probably had much to do with the success of its flights. Even at the risk of some repetition, another paragraph[2] is here quoted:

As *rigid* aeroplanes and screws were employed in the construction of these models (previously described) they flew in a hap-hazard sort of a way,

---

[1] It will occur to the reader that the flight of a sparrow is not conspicuous for its horizontality. Any one who experiments with motorless gliders (see AERONAUTICAL ANNUAL, No. 1, p. 166) made on the Pénaud principle will find the first flights decidedly sparrow-like, but he will also find that by varying the amount of weight carried, the position of the centre of gravity, and the size and angle of the rudder, the undulation of the flights can be made less and less. — *Ed.*

[2] See Encyclopædia Britannica, 9th edition, N.Y., 1879, Vol. IX., p. 321. The italics used in the quotation are in the original.

it being found exceedingly difficult to confer on them the necessary degree of stability fore and aft and laterally. M. Pénaud succeeded in overcoming the difficulty in question by the invention of what he designates his automatic rudder. This consists of a small *elastic* aeroplane placed aft or behind the principal aeroplane, which is also *elastic*. The two elastic aeroplanes extend horizontally and make a slight upward angle with the horizon, the angle made by the smaller aeroplane (the rudder) being slightly in excess of that made by the larger.

As there are several more subjects to be considered in this editorial, more space must not be given to this matter of automatic stability. To say that experiments with models can instruct us concerning it, is almost like stating an axiom.

We come now to the second subject: the disposition of surfaces. The nature of the questions which arise in this connection can best be explained by referring the reader to the previous pages of this number of THE ANNUAL, where Mr. Chanute has described the permutations of his surfaces,[1] and where Mr. Herring has discussed the matter of "interference."[2]

Very much of what is now known concerning the disposition of surfaces has been learned from the flights of models. I think that no experimenter will doubt that there is still more to be learned.

When we consider the third subject, the placing of screws, we shall see how models may instruct us in such a manner that undue risks of life and limb may be greatly lessened. The motorless gliding model is acted upon by two forces — gravity and the pressure of the air upon its surfaces. When a motor and propellers are used there is a third force, the thrust of the screws, which has to be considered in all calculations. We are justified in assuming that any self-propelled flying machine must have the excellence of equilibrium of the best gliding machine when at any time its engines are stopped; therefore it is possible to gain knowledge as to the best way of placing the *motor*, by using, in place of the motor, ballast having the weight and general form of the motor which is later to be used.

Where the line of screw-thrust is to come, so that, when this third force is applied, the equilibrium of the machine will not be

---

[1] See p. 35 *et seq.*     [2] See p. 63 *et seq.*

seriously compromised, is a matter upon which engineers are not fully agreed, and therefore an amateur may well refrain from expressing an opinion.   The difficulty comes in the travel of the centre of air pressure, which is now imperfectly understood.

This much seems probable, that if engineers will furnish working hypotheses, careful laymen may test these in placing the screws on their models, and in that way do useful work.

The air-sailer who in flight first adds the thrust of a screw to the forces he is accustomed to deal with will stand in need of all the knowledge which can be gained from self-propelled models.

The fourth subject is, the curves of surfaces.   Lilienthal's article entitled " The Best Shapes for Wings," which is given on previous pages, leaves at present little to say under this head.

The fifth and sixth subjects may be considered together.

The relation of the whole weight of a model to the area of its sustaining surfaces and the relation of the power used to the whole weight sustained are very important matters, and it may be assumed that when model-flying becomes common, many models will be made with removable motors, so that with one motor comparative tests of different forms of models can be made, and useful if not precise data be obtained.

The value of comparative tests made with steam motors would perhaps be impaired by the variations of the power coming from different conditions of the flame in different flights, but with compressed air or liquid carbonic acid the comparative tests would be useful, to say the least.

The seventh subject — the effects of elasticity in sustaining surfaces — gives great scope to experimenters.   Those who devote themselves to it can surely help to answer the still unanswered question, Does the feather structure of a bird's wing give to it a certain quality which makes it a better model for us to follow than the featherless wing of the bat?   To Lilienthal this seemed to be an open question.

I have tried to make a strong plea in behalf of the flying model.   It seems to me that, whatever its limitations may be, it can lessen the risks to life and limb.   We are fortunate that we live in a time of peace, when such things are the first to be thought of. If we were at war it would be necessary to call for recruits who would risk their lives in making glides from captive balloons, for if we did not do that some other nation would, and when bags of explosives are dropped into the smoke-stacks of multi-million-dollar battle-ships, it will cause a revision of opinions concerning the balance of power of the world.

## MOTIVE POWER FOR FLYING MODELS.

THE designer of a motor for a flying model must begin by choosing his type. There are not more than eight from which he is likely to choose. These are as follows: Motors actuated by (1) steam, (2) explosion of gas or vapor mixed with air, (3) electricity, (4) compressed air, (5) liquid carbonic acid, (6) rubber under torsion or tension, (7) steel springs, (8) inertia of a revolving body.

In choosing the type the designer will naturally, at the start, consider this question: What are the qualities most to be desired in the motor of a flying model? It goes without saying that it is desirable to have a maximum of power with a minimum of weight, and to have the motor safe to use. The other points to be considered are:

1. Probable usefulness of an enlarged counterpart.
2. Uniformity of motion.
3. Duration of action in flight.
4. Durability.
5. Economy.
6. Simplicity.

In considering types we may narrow the subject by a process of elimination.

Rubber under torsion or tension has the advantage of being extremely simple and cheap. It has the disadvantage of requiring the use of a fusee or something equally clumsy and wasteful of power if it is to give a uniform motion to a propeller. Pénaud, who died seventeen years ago, did excellent work with rubber-propelled models without using the fusee, yet it is probable that those who read what Dr. Langley says of rubber on pages 15 and 16 of this ANNUAL will conclude that while rubber may be useful for preliminary experiments, it is not likely to be so beyond these.

Makers of models who have experimented both with rubber and steel springs pronounce the latter to be inferior to the former.

Coming now to electricity, it is safe to say that the weight of any battery, primary or secondary, at present known, is too great to be carried by any flying machine. It has been suggested that experiments with models propelled by electric motors and furnished with energy through trailed conducting wires would be useful, but even a slack wire would be a disturbing element, and the phenomena observed would not be those of free flight.

The principle of inertia propulsion has been used to some extent in marine torpedoes. The highest velocity compatible with the strength of materials is given to a revolving wheel with a heavy rim; this wheel is like that of the gyroscope of the physical laboratories; in torpedoes it gives its energy to the propelling screws. Some experimenters have suggested the use of the gyroscope for giving stability to flying machines in horizontal flight. If this principle were applied in a flying model the wheel would serve a double purpose, if revolved in a horizontal plane and geared to propellers; that is, it would act to preserve the equilibrium of the model and also as a reservoir of energy. It seems to me that this method of propulsion offers less to the experimenter than those which are now to be considered.

In trying to accurately estimate the relative values of steam and explosion engines for our purpose, we must bear in mind the fact that during two centuries of experiment, the former have received much more attention from inventors than the latter. It is not necessary now to consider the reasons for this; it must suffice to say that the steam-engine is given into our hands in a comparatively well-matured condition, while the explosion-engine comes to us less fully developed. I think it will be generally admitted that the explosion-engine has at the present time greater possibilities of improvement than the steam-engine has.

It is speaking within bounds to say that as an authority on light-weight motors, Mr. Hiram S. Maxim stands second to no man in the world. His commendation of petroleum motors on p. 147 of No. 2 of THE ANNUAL should therefore be read with interest by students. In this connection, however, it is well to remember that the greatest successes ever made with light-weight motors have been made by Langley and Maxim respectively with steam-engines.[1]

In coming now to the consideration of motors moved by compressed air and liquid carbonic acid, it is necessary for a moment to refer to steam-motors as forming with them a group, and to note the fact that between these three types of motors there is such a strong similarity that in case we are compelled to abandon one form of energy and adopt another in its place, we can do so without making very radical changes in the motors. This would seem to be an advantage to experimenters.

If compressed air or liquid carbonic acid have any advantages over steam, I think that these would hold only in the case of the motor of a flying model, and that they would not be found in its enlarged counterpart. The reason for this opinion will be seen when we consider the relative length of flight of a flying model and that of a practical flying machine of man-carrying size. In the former a two-minute flight is ample, for at the end of that time the flying model will be at such a distance from the experimenter that observation and study of its conduct will be of little use. Of the latter a long flight is required.

With a small tubular holder for the air or carbonic acid it is possible to get a considerable amount of power for a short time, and this will suffice for very instructive flights of models. As to the comparative merits of liquid carbonic acid and compressed air, the reader is referred to the article which Pro-

[1] See p. 20 of this ANNUAL, p. 36 of No. 2 ANNUAL, and p. 444 *et seq.* "Century Magazine," N.Y., Jan., 1895.

fessor Peabody has kindly contributed to this number of THE ANNUAL. (See p. 147.)

As to a holder for the liquid carbonic acid or compressed air, it seems to me that it will be well to begin with one which will have about forty cubic inches of space. The only way that I know of to get a suitable holder is to have several made by a maker of the best shot-gun barrels, and then carry them to the hydraulic testers and have one-half of the lot tested to destruction; the other half should be tested to a sufficient degree to make them safe to transport when charged with liquid carbonic acid.

In conclusion it may be said that to the experimenter with flying models there are four types of motors which are likely to be useful; namely, the steam, explosion, compressed air, and carbonic acid motors. Each has advantages. As for immediate needs it seems to me that the air or carbonic acid motors are likely to be the most satisfactory, because they are comparatively simple and are sufficient for short flights.

------

## AN IMPORTANT WORK.

JUST as knowledge of the ocean currents is requisite in marine navigation, so knowledge of aerial currents is indispensable to those who would come to a right understanding of the problems of aeronautics.

Langley, in his "Internal Work of the Wind," has shown the importance of the pulsation of wind currents as a factor in explaining the phenomena of soaring flight; Chanute, Lilienthal, Maxim, Pénaud, and others have alluded to the ascending air currents which are now known to exist; Chanute and Herring on previous pages of this number of THE ANNUAL write of the rolling billows of air which they have encountered, and the result of all is, that we thirst for more knowledge concerning the mysterious aerial ocean.

The value of the data which have been gathered at Blue Hill Observatory in the past twelve years is known and appreciated by meteorologists in all parts of the world; yet now no longer content even with his summit station, the founder and director is making observations at altitudes of over 9,000 feet. The methods of work and the results so far reached are described elsewhere in this number of THE ANNUAL. The work is now well under way, and the knowledge which will be gained in the next few years is likely to prove of great value.

The Blue Hill Meteorological Observatory was built in 1885, by A. Lawrence Rotch, Esq., who has since directed its work and defrayed the cost of maintenance. This amounts now to over $4,000 a year. The observations and investigations have been published annually since 1887 in the "Annals of the Astronomical Observatory of Harvard College."

The situation of Mr. Rotch's observatory on the summit of the highest hill[1] in the vicinity of Boston, with a free exposure in all directions, especially adapts it to the needs of meteorologists.

The observations were first made in coöperation with the New England Meteorological Society. Among the methods and investigations which, proving successful at Blue Hill, were afterwards adopted by the United States Signal Service, and by its successor the United States Weather Bureau, there may be mentioned simple self-recording instruments with which the observatory was equipped in 1885 and 1886, the issue of local weather predictions, the international form of publishing meteorological data, observations of the height and velocity of clouds. Kites for elevating self-recording instruments which have been in use at Blue Hill since 1894 are about to be applied to this purpose by the United States Weather Bureau.

Since 1886 observations of the direction of motion and relative velocity of clouds have been made several times a day at Blue Hill, this being the longest series of the kind in the United States. Trigonometrical measurements of cloud heights and absolute velocities had been made in Sweden, and in 1890 and 1891 these were repeated at Blue Hill by Messrs. Clayton and Fergusson. The publication of the results obtained attracted

---

[1] The summit is 635 feet above sea level. It is 10.4 miles S.S.W. from the State House in Boston. Travellers from New York to Boston via Providence may see the observatory on the right about 15 minutes before reaching Boston. See illustration, Plate X.

much attention and facilitated the international scheme of cloud observation now being carried out, in which the instruments and methods employed six years previously at Blue Hill are again being used there.   It will be seen that such observations make known the direction and velocity of the air currents at different altitudes.

Of special interest to students of aeronautics are Mr. Fergusson's researches on the methods of measuring the horizontal and vertical components of the wind.   Kites furnish a new and important method of continuing these investigations in the free air at considerable heights above the earth's surface.   As these researches are carried farther, and as more becomes known concerning the vertical component measured above the greatly disturbed surface stratum, the ascending currents will not remain the almost unknown quantities which they now are.   To study these is to undertake a very difficult task; special instruments must be invented and constructed; yet from what has been done so far by Mr. Rotch and his able assistants, we are led to look for even more.

## KOCH'S APPARATUS.

THE accompanying drawings are reproduced from a plate dated November, 1889, and included in a pamphlet by Gustav Koch, published in Munich in 1891.   The title is " Free Human Flight as a Prerequisite of Dynamic Aeronautics."

Koch's drawings are given here solely because of the interest which attaches to them on account of his operator's position.

Not only was Koch ahead of his time when, in 1889, he suggested this horizontal position, but any man who might now advocate its immediate adoption would be too advanced. The control of the gliding machine, although becoming greater every year, is not yet sufficient to make it reasonably safe for an air-sailer to assume this position.

All this, however, need not prevent us from considering the great economy of power[1] which will result when, in the future,

---

[1] See AERONAUTICAL ANNUAL, No. 1, pp. 151-153.  See also Langley's " Experiments in Aerodynamics," p. 106, lines 33-40.

man shall acquire such control over the gliding machine that he can properly direct one of a very compact design while he occupies the position shown in the drawings.

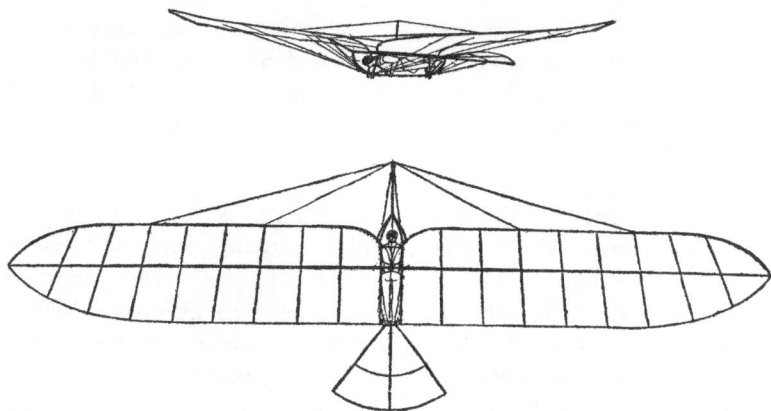

In the original drawing there are dotted lines to show how the position of the wings may be changed by swinging them backward and forward, thus changing the position of centre of pressure relatively to the centre of gravity. These lines do not appear in this cut. Mr. Chanute discusses Koch's device on pp. 215–217 of "Progress in Flying Machines."

THE length of time which it will take to reach a complete solution of the problem of mechanical flight will depend largely upon the amount of money contributed to pay the expenses of experimenters.

Money so contributed may easily be wasted, and there are never wanting men who eagerly affirm that a certain amount of money placed in their hands will surely bring the solution of the problem.

If some Lorenzo di Medici should now appear near the close of this nineteenth century, his first thought concerning this subject would be, " If I give a large sum of money for the purpose of bringing to the nineteenth century the credit of achieving mechanical flight, how can I assure myself that the money will be wisely used? "

The Editor suggests this answer to the question: Let any donor make his gift to science with one condition; namely, that the faculties of the four leading technological institutes of the United States shall consent to choose a board of five trustees who shall control all the expenditures of the fund. This would be a sure safeguard against incompetent claimants.

---

WHEN a model glider with a Pénaud rudder is heavily weighted it ordinarily requires a high starting point to give it velocity sufficient to sustain the weight; the large angle at which the rudder is set makes a long swoop necessary before the model steers itself into a horizontal course. Sometimes a sufficiently high launching place is not attainable. Query: Can good glides be made from a comparatively low starting point by setting the tail at a smaller angle with the main sustaining surfaces, and arranging it to snap back into the large angle position two or three seconds after launching? A spring released by the unwinding of a rubber cord might answer the purpose.

---

MR. R. W. WOOD was one of the last Americans to visit Lilienthal and to witness his flights. On Sunday, Aug. 2, 1896, just one week before the fatal accident, he was at Rhinow hills with the dauntless engineer. In the "Boston Evening Transcript" of Saturday, Oct. 31, 1896 (page 20), will be found a very interesting article of two columns' length in which Mr. Wood tells the story.

---

IT having been stated in the public prints that THE AERO-NAUTICAL ANNUAL is published under the auspices of the Boston Aeronautical Society, the Editor wishes to say that it never was so published, and, further, that he has ceased to be a member of the society referred to, and knows nothing of its proceedings. None of the resident members of that society are now contributors to the pages of THE ANNUAL.

THE illustrations on Plates III., V., and XV. are made from drawings kindly contributed by Robert D. Andrews, Esq.

---

" McClure's Magazine" states that in a future number it will publish "the first authentic account" of Professor Langley's flying machine. The readers of THE ANNUAL will perceive that the statement is erroneous.

---

FLYERS of models may make progress by taking the best gliding machine of the previous season and reproducing it in a convenient working model size and applying motor and screws to it.

---

THE records of the Aeronautical Society of Great Britain show that Otto Lilienthal was a member as early as 1873.

---

## AERONAUTICAL PERIODICALS.

*Zeitschrift für Luftschiffahrt und Physik der Atmosphäre.* — Edited by Dr. A. Berson. Published monthly by Mayer & Müller, Berlin. Subscription price (in Postal Union), 13 M. 50 Pf. per annum. Established 16 years.

*The Aeronautical Journal.* — Published quarterly at 2 s. per copy, by King, Sell & Railton, Ltd., 4, Bolt Court, Fleet St., London, E.C.

*L'Aéronaute.* — Edited by M. Hureau de Villeneuve. Monthly. Office of publication, 91 Rue d'Amsterdam, Paris. Subscription price (in Postal Union), 9 francs per annum. Established 30 years.

*L'Aérophile.* — Edited by M. George Besançon. Monthly. Office of publication, 14 Rue des Grandes-Carrières, Paris. Subscription price (in Postal Union), 12 francs per annum. Established 5 years.

*Revue de l'Aéronautique.* — Edited by M. Henri Hervé. Quarterly. Published by Masson et Cie., 120 B'd Saint Germain, Paris. Subscription price (in Postal Union), 10 francs per annum. Established 7 years.

STUDENTS who give especial attention to the subject of air resistances will be interested in the following work: *Die Luftwiderstandsgesetze, der Fall durch die Luft und der Vogelflug* (304 pp., 67 illus.), by Friedrich Ritter von Loessl. Published by A. Hölder, Vienna, 1895. A copy of this work has been received by THE ANNUAL; it was first loaned to a meteorologist, next to a professor of engineering, it is now in the hands of a physicist in Washington, and when returned it will be given to the Boston Public Library. The authors and publishers of scientific books and pamphlets may be sure that when copies are sent to THE ANNUAL they will be put to a good use.

THE date of issue of this, the third number of THE ANNUAL, is May 25, 1897. It was necessary this year to postpone publication in order to give the leading contributors ample time to complete their articles. Last year THE ANNUAL was published in February, and it is hoped that future numbers may appear in that month, so that experimenters may have more time to study the previous season's work before arranging their summer plans. Contributors will please send in their articles for No. 4 some time during November, 1897. Please address communications to THE EDITOR OF THE AERONAUTICAL ANNUAL, CARE OF W. B. CLARKE & CO., PARK ST., COR. TREMONT ST., BOSTON, MASS., U.S.A.

EXPERIMENTERS in all parts of the world are invited to send, for publication in the next number of The Annual, concise accounts of their experiments. Contributors will kindly note the following: 1. The Editor is not to be held responsible for rejected manuscripts, drawings, or photographs. 2. In describing experiments, contributors are requested to send photographs, and also working-drawings of those pieces of apparatus which they consider their best. 3. Well-illustrated descriptions of experiments with the following kinds of apparatus are especially desired: Gliding machines; Self-propelled models; Motors; Screw propellers. 4. All photographs should be distinct, or they cannot be satisfactorily reproduced. All drawings should be in very black ink on white paper or tracing-cloth, and they should be sufficiently well executed to be photo-engraved without re-drawing. 5. Accuracy, explicitness, and conciseness of statement are desirable in the extreme. 6. Please state if any of the text or illustrations have been in print before, and, if so, where. Please give dates of all experiments.

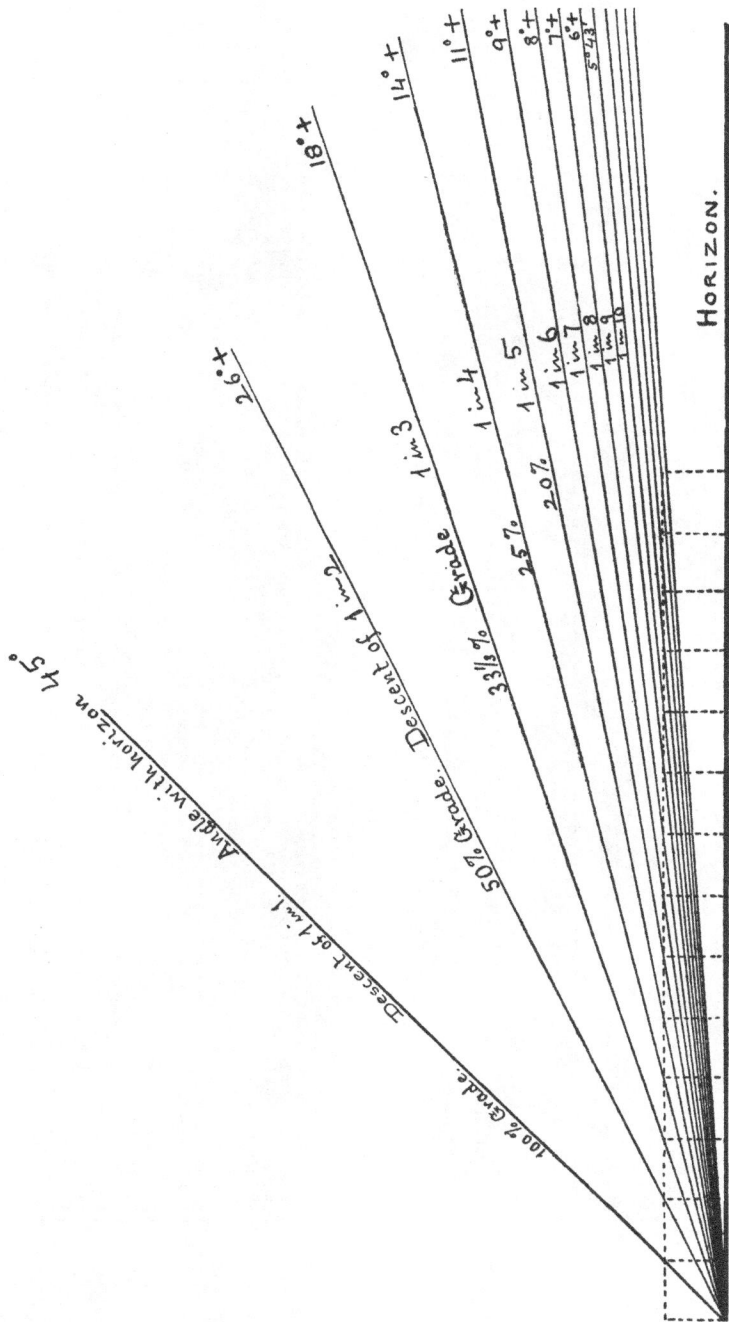

The above diagram is intended to assist the eye in judging the angle of descent of an air-sailing machine or gliding model.

Horizon.

+18°

+14°

+11°

+9°
+8°
+7°
+6°
5°43'

26°

Grade
1 in 4

1 in 5

1 in 6
1 in 7
1 in 8
1 in 9
1 in 10

33⅓% Grade
1 in 3

25%

20%

50% Grade. Descent of 1 in 2

Angle with horizon 45°

Descent of 1 in 1

100% Grade.

(177)

# HERRING'S TABLE.

Properties of a curved surface, curved to arc of a circle having a rise of arc equal to $1/12$ the breadth of wing, deduced from Lilienthal's tables and Smeaton's coefficient ($.005\ v^2$).

| Angle of incidence. | Lift, per cent. of normal plane. | Drift, as a per cent. of lift. | Max. travel horizontally for one foot fall. | Miles per hour for one lb. per sq. ft. | Mile pounds per lb. supported with loading of one lb. per sq. ft. | Pounds per horse-power. |
|---|---|---|---|---|---|---|
| —9 | .000 | inf. | 0 | inf. | inf. | 0 |
| —8 | .0396 | 1.54 | .65 | 71. | 109.34 | 3.43 |
| —7 | .0792 | .655 | 1.525 | 50.2 | 32.75 | 11.4 |
| —6 | .119 | .396 | 2.53 | 40.9 | 16.2 | 23.15 |
| —5 | .160 | .257 | 3.89 | 35.3 | 9.07 | 41.3 |
| —4 | .200 | .175 | 5.72 | 31.75 | 5.53 | 67.8 |
| —3 | .242 | .125 | 8.00 | 28.85 | 3.62 | 103.6 |
| —2 | .286 | .091 | 10.9 | 26.45 | 2.41 | 155.6 |
| —1 | .332 | .076 | 13.1 | 24.9 | 1.87 | 200.5 |
| 0 | .381 | .063 | 15.8 | 22.9 | 1.45 | 251.7 |
| +1 | .434 | .0544 | 18.4 | 21.5 | 1.17 | 320.6 |
| 2 | .489 | .0513 | 19.5 | 20.2 | 1.04 | 360.6 |
| 3 | .546 | .0525 | 19.0 | 19.1 | .993 | 377.6 |
| 4 | .600 | .0582 | 17.1 | 18.3 | 1.07 | 359.5 |
| 5 | .650 | .0655 | 15.2 | 17.54 | 1.14 | 329. |
| 6 | .689 | .0708 | 14.1 | 17.03 | 1.25 | 300. |
| 7 | .730 | .0850 | 15.2 | 16.55 | 1.41 | 266. |
| 8 | .764 | .0862 | 11.7 | 16.18 | 1.48 | 268. |
| 9 | .792 | .105 | 11.6 | 15.9 | 1.67 | 224.6 |
| 10 | .808 | .116 | 9.5 | 15.7 | 1.82 | 206.05 |
| 11 | .829 | .125 | 8.0 | 15.5 | 1.84 | 204. |
| 12 | .847 | .137 | 7.3 | 15.4 | 2.11 | 177.7 |
| 13 | .852 | .151 | 6.6 | 15.3 | 2.31 | 162.3 |
| 14 | .864 | .165 | 6.0 | 15.2 | 2.51 | 149.4 |
| 15 | .870 | .18 | 5.55 | 15.15 | 2.73 | 137.4 |
| 16 | .873 | .20 | 5. | 15.1 | 3.02 | 124.2 |
| 17 | .875 | .223 | 4.48 | 15.1 | 3.37 | 113.3 |
| 18 | .874 | .244 | 4.10 | 15.1 | 3.68 | 102.0 |
| 19 | .880 | .27 | 3.70 | 15.15 | 4.08 | 91.9 |
| 20 | .866 | .30 | 3.3 | 15.2 | 4.56 | 82.2 |
| 21 | .862 | .32 | 3.13 | 15.25 | 4.88 | 79.0 |
| 22 | .856 | .35 | 2.86 | 15.3 | 5.36 | 70.1 |
| 23 | .850 | .37 | 2.71 | 15.3 | 5.66 | 65.3 |
| 24 | .843 | .40 | 2.5 | 15.4 | 6.16 | 60.8 |
| 25 | .825 | .434 | 2.30 | 15.55 | 6.71 | 55.9 |
| 26 | .827 | .458 | 2.18 | 15.56 | 7.12 | 52.6 |
| 27 | .818 | .484 | 2.07 | 15.6 | 7.55 | 49.6 |
| 28 | .808 | .50 | 2.0 | 15.5 | 7.75 | 48.4 |
| 29 | .797 | .54 | 1.85 | 15.9 | 8.59 | 43.6 |
| 30 | .788 | .57 | 1.75 | 15.9 | 9.06 | 41.4 |
| 32 | .768 | .62 | 1.61 | 16.1 | 9.98 | 37.5 |
| 35 | .733 | .76 | 1.32 | 16.55 | 12.58 | 30. |
| 40 | .681 | .86 | 1.16 | 17.15 | 14.75 | 25.0 |
| 45 | .628 | 1.03 | .97 | 17.8 | 18.33 | 20.4 |
| 50 | .570 | 1.20 | .83 | 18.7 | 22.44 | 12.3 |
| 55 | .510 | 1.48 | .68 | 19.8 | 29.30 | 12.0 |
| 60 | .450 | 1.79 | .56 | 21.1 | 37.77 | 9.7 |
| 70 | .318 | 2.87 | .348 | 25.1 | 72.3 | 5.2 |
| 80 | .167 | 5.79 | .173 | 34.6 | 200.33 | 1.85 |
| 90 | 0 | inf. | 0 | inf. | inf. | 0 |

In the accompanying tables the first column is the angle of inclination of the chord in reference to the horizontal when the surface is moved through still air.

The second column is the proportion of ($.005\ v^2$) the normal pressure which acts as a lifting force at the velocity V in miles per hour. The result would be given in pounds per square foot of area. Thus one square foot of curved surface having a rise of arc of about one-twelfth of its chord length, if exposed at a positive angle of eight degrees in a wind of twenty miles an hour, would exert a lifting effect of $.005 \times 20 \times 20 \times .764 = 1.528$ pounds = say one and a half pounds per square foot.

The third column is the driving force necessary to overcome the resistance of the surface, it is expressed as a fraction of the weight resting on the surface. If this weight be (as before found) 1.528 pounds, then the driving force necessary is $1.528 \times .0862 = .1317$ pounds for every square foot of surface of the machine. If, however, the weight of a machine complete is known, and is, say, 200 pounds, and it is desired to find the push of the screws necessary to drive it at an angle of, say, 8 degrees, we can find the necessary thrust directly by multiplying the weight 200 pounds by the factor in the third column opposite 8 degrees, thus $200 \times .0862 = 17.24$ pounds, which is, however, probably not more than one-third the total resistance which should be allowed on any practical machine. The fourth column is the reciprocal of the third-column figures. It shows how far a surface would travel (theoretically), given in terms of the height lost. Thus a surface would travel 19.5 feet horizontally for every foot fallen through—if the surface be maintained at an angle of 2 degrees with the relative wind. The fifth column is the speed necessary to support one pound per square foot at the given angle. Thus at a positive angle of 2 degrees it would require a speed of 20.2 miles per hour to sustain an apparatus when the total load on it was just one pound for every square foot of sustaining surface. The other columns scarcely need explanation. In computing the normal pressure of the wind, it is better in a full-sized machine to compute the natural wind as $.005\ v^2$, and with the apparatus moved in still air to use the formula $.004\ v^2$, as the effect in moving through still air is much less than that produced by the natural wind of the same velocity. The greater pressure of the natural wind is the logical effect of its irregularity, for the *mean of the squares* of several different velocities is easily proven to be greater than *the square* of their *mean velocity.*

NOTE. The lift and drift and mile pounds for 1°, 3°, 4°, 11°, 16°, 19°, and 20° have been very closely verified by experiments of A. M. Herring with a small regulated kite of 3 square feet.

www.ingramcontent.com/pod-product-compliance
Lightning Source LLC
Chambersburg PA
CBHW031251090426
42742CB00007B/413